Praise for *Lessons from the Cloth 2: 501 More One Minute Motivators for Leaders*

Once again, my friends Bo Prosser and Charles Qualls have opened the window to authentic leadership by offering some outstanding thoughts on leadership. Some of the ideas are drawn from others, but most of this list reflects the wisdom and insight of two special people. If you are like me, you will pause at almost every idea and ponder deeply how this can make each of us a more compassionate person and effective leader.

—**Charles Bugg**
Leadership Consultant for CBF and Adjunct Professor of Leadership at Baptist Seminary of Kentucky

This book provides leaders with important reminders of ways to lead effectively and with wisdom. The encouragement to make space for the Holy, integrate prayer into the daily routine, and practice forgiveness are wise counsel for Christians in leadership.

—**Margaret Campbell**
Chair, Renovaré Board of Trustees

Leadership does not just happen; it is the result of planning and execution. The motivational thoughts contained here will keep you focused on the right things and positioned at the front of the pack, right where leaders belong.

—**Larry Carroll**
Carroll Financial, Charlotte, North Carolina

These one-minute motivators allow me to carry around executive leadership coaching wisdom in my briefcase! Two areas of content that are especially useful to me:

1. Creativity motivators allow us to expand our perceptions, which enables us to take the perspectives of others. Without creativity we are dead in the water as leaders.

2. Asking the right questions allows us to think critically as leaders; these motivators are full of provocative and relevant questions.

Well done, Prosser and Qualls—thanks for a wonderful tool!

—**Pamela Emerson Ey**
Founder of The Center for Innovative Decision Making

Leadership can be deeply rewarding, filled with joy, exceedingly stressful, and exhausting—sometimes simultaneously. This collection of wise sayings about leadership is like a box of mixed chocolates, each self-contained and capable of giving micro-respite from the tasks at hand and of re-energizing to face those tasks. Some bring smiles of recognition; others are reorienting, like seeing a signpost beside a road otherwise obscured by thick fog. Be sure to have a highlighter or sticky notes at the ready to mark those that you will want to come back to again and again.

—**Diana Garland**
Dean and Professor, Baylor University School of Social Work

These practical nuggets of wisdom gleaned from within congregational life by Prosser and Qualls, both veteran practitioners of ministry, may prove more valuable to church and community leaders than a library filled with volumes on leadership theory.

—**Barry Howard**
Pastor, First Baptist Church of Pensacola

The first volume of *501 One Minute Motivators for Leaders* is a valuable resource that offers guidance each time I take a minute to read a tip. Adding another 501 tips, with this new book, provides even more insights and inspiration for leaders. Prosser and Qualls provide practical, forthright, concise, easy-to-employ thoughts about life. I highly recommend this for all of us; we are all leaders in some facet of life.

—**Eric Hyman**
Athletic Director, Texas A & M University

What leader isn't looking for succinct summaries of timeless principles? As anyone knows who's ever read Dag Hammarskjöld's *Markings*, the poetry of Robert Frost, or especially the book of Proverbs, axioms bring precision and clarity to any decision-making process. This book, like the volume before it, is an enormously valuable addition to the leader's toolbox.

—**Julie Pennington Russell**
Pastor, First Baptist, Decatur, Georgia

LESSONS FROM THE CLOTH — 2

501 MORE ONE MINUTE MOTIVATORS FOR LEADERS

BO PROSSER and CHARLES QUALLS

Lessons from the Cloth 2
501 More One Minute Motivators for Leaders

Bo Prosser
Charles Qualls

Lessons from the Cloth 2
501 More One Minute Motivators for Leaders

Bo Prosser, Charles Qualls

© 2013 Smyth & Helwys Publishing, Inc.
6316 Peake Road
Macon, Georgia 31210-3960
1-800-747-3016

All rights reserved.
Printed in the United States of America.

The paper used in this publication
meets the minimum requirements of American National
Standard for Information Sciences—Permanence of Paper
for Printed Library Materials, ANSI Z39.48–1984.

Library of Congress Cataloguing-in-Publication Data

Prosser, Bo.
    Lessons from the cloth 2: 501 more one-minute motivators for leaders/Bo Prosser, Charles Qualls.
    p. cm.
    ISBN 978-1-57312-665-6 (pbk.)
    1. Leadership.
    2. Leadership—Religious aspects—Christianity.
    I. Qualls, Charles. II. Title.
    BF637.L4P66 1999
    262'1—dc21   98-30883
                                                                        CIP

My heartfelt love and appreciation…
To all those wise people in my life who have challenged me to think and to all those loving people in my life who have loved me when I wasn't thinking!
To those who've called me to follow and to those who've challenged me to lead.
Especially to Gail, Jamie and Justin, Katie and Sean for your grace and unconditional love.

—BRP

My deepest love and thanks...
For those who have taken the time and energy to guide me, and who continue to.
For the congregations who have learned these lessons alongside me, and sometimes way ahead!
For the gift of devoted friends and talented co-workers who are invaluable companions.
And, mostly to Elizabeth who loves me through it all!

—CLQ

Preface

Aldous Huxley supposedly said that a bad book is as much of a labor to write as a good one. Here, then, is the fruit of our labor. Our labor on this "good book" began a few months ago. We've worked hard in our research, and what follows is the result of time spent in personal reflection and professional interaction. We bring you 501 *more* one-minute motivators that represent the best of those personal and collegial insights.

We are building upon the success of our previous volume, *501 One Minute Motivators for Leaders*, and we hope this book will capture the same spirit of leadership and personal growth within many of you that the original volume did. Thus, we labor to write another volume. Our labor has brought the book to publication; the quality of the book depends on your response.

We are laboring to make this a good book—actually, a great book! But we are not laboring for our own satisfaction. We write because leadership is at a crucial point in churches, corporations, families, and almost every arena of life. Leadership is the force that drives organizations to accomplishment. Without leadership there is chaos. *With* leadership there is sometimes chaos. We hope to share with you some motivational thoughts on good leadership, positive leadership—leadership that adds to the common good.

As was true with the first volume, we began this work to advise a mutual friend who was just entering leadership in congregational ministry. He was brand new and knew very little about being a leader. And so we wrote for him, distilling our own thoughts about leadership. We soon found ourselves with a book full of motivational thoughts. These are some of the thoughts that have kept us focused in our own ministries, management experiences, personal relationships, and even our marriages. Based on the response to volume one, we're back with another 501 thoughts based on our experiences, readings, and research. Take these, make them your own, and lead on bravely.

There are many theories about leading, leadership development, and leadership traits. These motivators are not fashioned around any school of leadership, any theory of leadership, or any particular leadership style. What we are sharing comes from years of experience in the trenches leading congregations, organizations, and relationships. We are sharing what we live and what we love.

The one special motivator that keeps us focused is, "People go where they know they've been prepared for and are cared for." (We know it's not good grammar, but we know it is good leadership.) People are our most important resource. One cannot be a leader without followers! Leadership is about developing healthy relationships to work together to accomplish a mission. The thoughts that follow will hopefully spur you on to build your own teams, grow your own healthy relationships, and break through to new heights in your own leadership.

Enjoy the journey. Make marks in the margins. Highlight those that have special meaning for you. Write your own motivators in the back of the book on the extra pages supplied. Have some fun! Not all of these motivators are offered for serious intellectual and philosophical debate. Some of them are offered just because they've helped us "lighten up" and enjoy the work that was before us. We hope upon reading that you feel inspired, encouraged, and maybe a bit "enter-trained."

#1 Knowing yourself better is the beginning of knowing others. When you are less mystified by who you are, you can begin to notice the important things about others around you.

#2 What is your "breath prayer"? Develop a short prayer that coincides with your breathing. As you inhale, think of a short phrase to recite internally. As you exhale, think of another short phrase to recite internally. Repeat the phrases during the day each time you become aware of your breathing. For instance, as you inhale, "Stay focused, stay focused. . . ." As you exhale, "Be intentional, be intentional. . . ." As you begin each day, ask yourself, "What is my breath prayer today?" Live into the discipline of "praying as you breathe" each day.

#3 "Listen to experts, but be wary when they all rally around consensus."
      —Larry Carroll, Carroll Financial

#4 Self-knowledge is a moving target. We change throughout the days of our lives. Allow honesty within yourself. Allow honesty for others to see too!

#5 Sometimes you have to "unlearn" before you can "relearn." Sometimes you have to slow down to be able to move fast. Trust the process and live in the moment, keeping focused on your goals.

#6 The way you look at situations (relationships, yourself) determines what you see. If you look and always see problems, you work from a problem-solving mode. If you look and always see possibilities, you work with creativity and hope.

#7 Organizations are generally change-resistant by nature unless designed (probably recently) with *change* as a built-in value. At the systemic level, change is viewed as an "intruder" and is problematic. At the institutional level, change is viewed as an aggravation and is almost prohibited. How does your organizational culture view change? How can you become a change-agent without being viewed as an intruder or aggravator?

#8 One of the most important life passages for adults is accepting who you are. Grieve the things you are not; celebrate the things you are. Get on with being who you are. Work out of your passion for living and serving.

#9 Change the way people think about an issue by introducing them to a person who is affected by the issue. An issue with a "face" is personal and no longer just an ambiguous debate.

#10 Friend and leadership author Doug Grady says that he is often dislodged from being *stuck* when he hears his father's voice inside himself: "Do it anyway, son." Got a powerful case of the I-don't-wannas? *Do it anyway.* Have something you are dreading? *Do it anyway.* Held back by uncertainty? *Do it anyway.* Afraid someone will be a little upset by the action you know you have to take? *Do it anyway.* Stop being stuck!

#11 Prayer is some of the most important "personal work" you can do. Spend some quiet time each day focusing on how the divine is within you, around you, and leading you. Prayer is a discipline that has to be practiced daily.

#12 Work on the parts of you that need improvement. Accept the parts of you that don't work so well, but can be left alone. Make peace with yourself.

#13 It seems that Jesus was not that impressed with old wineskins. The more you work among them, the more you understand why. The trick is moving intentionally to the new in a way that builds collaboration. (Thanks, Shane McNary!)

#14 Believing that others can (and do!) like you is a vital part of the life-journey. So many leaders actively struggle with insecurity, lovability, and acceptance. Don't manipulate relationships or violate your own integrity to be liked. Take note, though, when others send positive affirmations your way. Take them to heart!

#15 If you don't know what time it is, you will not be constrained by time. Some projects require large chunks of time. Put your watch away and focus on the project. Feel the thrill of accomplishment.

#16 Those who think themselves needed rarely are. Those who think themselves important are usually less so than they think. Those who think themselves just "normal" are usually more needed and important than they realize.

#17 We need water. Drink 6 to 8 glasses per day. Drink from an intellectual fountain daily, too. Also drink some Holy Water from time to time. Stay healthy physically, emotionally, and spiritually, caring for your body, mind, and soul.

#18 Stay alert! Nothing runs on autopilot forever. Stay in touch with leadership and keep relationships strong.

#19 The successful leader seems to be some magical mixture of acute analyst, avid scholar, careful listener, astute historian, tenacious riverboat gambler, voracious reader, and life-long learner.
—Paraphrased from Barton Briggs, investment manager, Morgan Stanley

#20 There is no single factor that makes a successful leader, and even people with the right tools must want to grow, learn, and explore new ideas.

#21 You don't know what you don't know! Surround yourself with people who can advise you and keep you informed. Remind yourself that there is still a lot to learn.

#22 You cannot tell by looking at people what their demons are. You have to spend time listening and building deep relationships to help. Relationships are key no matter what the arena.

#23 Secrets are dangerous! Be careful what knowledge you protect. Be careful what relationships you enter into secretly.

#24 Challenges present opportunities to be empowered beyond the challenges!

#25 Take time to make friends with folks in each generation in your church. The main difference between a "twenty-something" and a "fifty-something" is that some "twenty-somethings" feel entitled to that which took the "fifty-somethings" twenty years to attain.

#26 While your ego is clamoring to speak up, get in touch with your empathy instead. Or allow your sympathy to surface as needed. Empathy and sympathy will inevitably guide you to healthier leadership destinations than the ego. Let your heart speak louder than your insecurity.

#27 A healthy leader is a better leader. One part of health is accepting some of the basics of who you are. We can exercise our souls and our personalities just as we exercise our bodies. Take time to pray, discern, be nicer, and more attentive. What do you need to do in order to rebalance the weaker parts of you?

#28 Why would you trust yourself? Are you more gifted and smarter than others? Are you so accomplished that there can simply be no doubt anymore? If your ego is leading this, proceed cautiously. If your personal development and growth is revealing this, move with confidence.

#29   Be careful whom you trust. Know them, test them. Watch them and help them. If you do trust them, then follow that trail of trust to see where it leads.

#30   Do you know how to *play?* Every so often, your team needs to play together. If you are someone who doesn't naturally do this, find a team member who does. Anoint them to be your organization's unofficial "manager of fun." Turn them loose to plan an occasional fun time instead of a staff meeting.

#31   The trust you are given when new in an organization pales in comparison with the trust you will earn if you lead with vision and integrity.

#32   There once was a leader. She wasn't the most physically commanding person in the organization. She wasn't always the loudest. But she showed up every day and consistently added excellence and integrity to the office. She was a most effective leader because her coworkers knew they could depend on her. What about you?

#33 "We forgive in pieces."

—Unknown

#34 Forgiveness is not merely an oath or an intention. Forgiveness is not a moment, a promise, or a ceremony. Forgiveness is infinitely harder than that, and can take a while to unfold. Forgiveness is letting go, forgetting, and moving forward with a clean slate, clear conscience, and comforted relationship.

#35 Forgiveness is like peeling back the layers of an onion. With one insight, one action, and one change at a time, we move closer to the flavorful center.

#36 Pray with a spirit of forgiveness as part of your daily quiet time. If you can pray forgiving those who have wronged you, you free your energy to focus on your own spiritual growth.

#37 "Jazz will endure as long as people hear it through their feet instead of their brains."
—John Philip Sousa

#38 Do you work with a skill set or a bag of tricks? The difference is critical. The skill set works from a creative approach to continued exploration. The bag of tricks uses the "same old, same old" over and over. One is fresh; one is tired. One is energizing; one is boring.

#39 One friend shared his conviction that a leader only has "tricks" to last for about three years. Guess how long this leader's tenure has been at most stops in his career? You guessed it: about three years. If you have skills, you can live in the moment, be continually creative, and outlive the tendency to give in to boredom.

#40 The creative leader is one who can move from day to day, assignment to assignment, and project to project, thriving on ambiguity, enjoying the creative process, and reinventing solutions without a loss of enthusiasm.

#41 Are you someone who expresses your appreciation? This aptitude does not come easily for all of us. Develop the ability to recognize and affirm a job well done or relationship much appreciated. Say "thanks" to a valued team member, friend, or family member. Express your gratitude!

#42 What is threatening the morale of your team? Research has long indicated that having a valued job, receiving a paycheck, or holding a responsible position is not sufficient for motivating your team members. Find out what does motivate your team and respond appropriately.

#43 What builds the morale of your team? To the extent that you can find out what really motivates them, try to give your team intentional doses of what you discover. Sure, this requires a little extra effort—but the payoff is big.

#44 When the hurt is too deep, forgiveness might seem to take so long that you begin to doubt whether the relationship is worth preserving. Forgiveness can take a while, but should not be forsaken!

#45 We communicate for a lot of different reasons. Be careful that you know how to translate the communication that comes your way.

#46 A question is not always a question. A statement is not always a statement. What makes the difference? Find out. But be careful how you find out!

#47 Some humor is serious. Sometimes things said in jest are meant to make a point. Listen attentively to distinguish the subtle differences between joking and teaching.

#48 Some humor is hurtful. Sometimes things said in jest are meant to hurt or harm. Be careful when joking that you are sharing humor appropriately—neither to harm nor to correct.

#49 You don't need a whole piece of paper to articulate one idea. Think about a "bumper sticker" thought or a short elevator-ride speech. Sell the idea and explain it along the way.

#50 Only *you* can build respect for you. Develop a bit of a thick skin, acquire the ability to laugh at yourself and with others, stay positive in the midst of negatives, and be persistent. If you don't respect yourself, don't expect others to do so.

#51 There are those who will try not to take responsibility for their words. Indeed, communication is a three-step process with the speaker, the hearer, and feedback (or resulting action). As the speaker, I am responsible for the explicit and implicit meanings of what I say.

#52 Psychologists argue that our strongest concepts of self must come from within. If so, we must do our own self-management and maintenance. Technically, they are right. But we still need to hear affirmations from those who lead us. We need praise and support. Give thanks, affirmation, and praise to those who earn it!

#53 One leader insisted that those who reported to him didn't need annual evaluation, that they didn't need to get any "attaboys" from him. He said, "If you are in trouble with me—you'll know it!" Those he supervised thirsted for something . . . anything . . . of praise from him. You can do better than this.

#54 George Bernard Shaw warns that churches must learn humility as well as teach it. The same goes for your church, corporation, office, or particular setting.

#55 "To do anything of magnitude takes at least five years, more likely seven or eight."
—Steve Jobs

#56 Not all communication involves the same levels of risk and emotion. Be sure you know how to speak multiple "languages" of the head and heart. Your leadership will be the better for this.

#57 Often, introverts have a difficult time in the workplace because the extroverts are so gregarious. Value the person who quietly, confidently goes about their work with quality and persistence.

#58 Your workplace is a team. The pressing question is this: *What kind of team is yours?* Some teams play together better than others.

#59 There once was an all-star player. However, he lacked a winning trait: nothing about his brilliant play elevated any of his teammates to a higher level. He remained baffled by his bad luck of being on teams that didn't win much. Maybe he wasn't as brilliant a player as everyone thought.

#60 Teams can function in a healthy manner, enjoying a synergy that produces creative results—good results that lead to observations such as "the sum is greater than the parts." Teams can also lapse into cultures of dysfunction—the kind of dysfunction that keeps them from living up to their promise. Again, the question is this: *What kind of team is yours?*

#61 Are you modeling what you demand of others around you? It may not be very efficient if the CEO is scrubbing toilets; however, the team needs to know that the boss would be *willing* to do so, if necessary! That knowledge goes a long way within any leader's team.

#62   When beginning to bring change, understand that you might be the only one in the system who sees the need to change, improve, and grow. Bringing change will not be easy.

#63   When beginning to bring change, don't mistake enthusiasm for the "old ways" as resistance to the "proposed way." Some folks just want to see how committed *you* are before they jump on board with you!

#64   Don't wait until you are totally happy to engage in the magic of laughter! Find a way to laugh out loud at least once a day!

#65   Set measures for success or others will do so. Don't let the old measures of success keep you bound up. Set new metrics and communicate these clearly so all involved know how to help you succeed.

#66 There is no competition among lighthouses. A candle's light is not diminished by sharing flame to light another candle! Find a group of peers, learn from each other, grow together, and make your work meaningful.

#67 "Where you live should no longer determine whether you live, or whether you die."
—Bono

#68 What are you doing in your life to make a difference for those who have less in your community, in your area, in your world?

#69 People take on patterns of behaviors in relationships. Workplaces take on patterns, too. Which of the ingrained cultures in your organization serve you well? Which of them don't work so well and need to be transformed?

#70 Companies and organizations have unique personalities, just as people and families do. Your group will find that there are areas where you excel, just as there are areas that need some work.

#71 Learning to work as part of a team comes more naturally to some people than to others. As a leader, you will not be able to work in the same way with each individual. What works with some will absolutely not work with others. How diverse and creative are you as a leader?

#72 Are you willing to admit when you are wrong? Do your team members see you accept blame when you are part of the problem? Being "right" isn't always what good organizational leadership is all about. You can't be right all the time!

#73 Every day is a new adventure! Begin each day with the energy of an explorer living into the excitement of what each new adventure brings. Do you start the day with boredom or dread? Guess what kind of day you'll have?

#74 The occasional strategic or verbal misstep is much easier to overlook when your body of work is already speaking on your behalf. What is the sum of your effort? If you are a "marathoner," chances are your coworkers know how you fit into their team.

#75 Sprinters are impressive for a while, and every team needs a good sprinter. But organizations are ultimately built on marathoners. Which one are you?

#76 Do you try to lead your team as though every member holds an equal position of power and value? This sounds nice because human beings have equal inherent value. But is everyone of equal position and value? Doubtful. *You* are the leader; lead! Give people a voice, but rely on your position and the expertise of your direct reports.

#77 Leaders will use a lot of their workday in concert with others on their team. How they use that time will buy the capital—or expend precious resources—necessary to continue leading. Operating in a vacuum will not impress those you hope to lead.

#78 Ask good questions! "Questions have greater power to transform us than do straight-forward answers."
        —Trevor Hudson

#79 Your team, company, or organization needs to know itself. Being all things to all people is not a likely path to success. How does your group's "personality" shape its vision and purpose?

#80 We live in an age that has institutionalized consensus building. Not all things in life can be accomplished by a majority vote. At some point, visionary leaders have to "sell" their visions for others to embrace and support them.

#81 Know when to take a survey or lead a focus group; know when to trust your gut. Sometimes you need to check your bias with trusted advisers. But you can't gather information and advice about everything. That's just not practical.

#82 Is what you are doing getting you anywhere, or nowhere? Sometimes the starting place for change is admitting what we do not want to admit: take a positive step by owning up to the negative.

#83 Know how to filter feedback. Learn whom to listen to closely, and learn whom to listen to in passing. Filtering the feedback we receive can be quite wise. Instructional words challenge and build; inaccurate or slanted words only hold us back.

#84 Leadership takes on many forms and many voices. What is your own, unique voice of leadership? Owning that voice may be a key to discovering your own power.

#85 We lead in diverse ways. Some lead quietly, while some are quite boisterous. Some lead by challenging, and some by inspiring. Some lead by bullying, some by their own confidence. How do you lead?

#86 God has called us to be humble. But God does not necessarily call us to "play small" just because we value humility. How can you reconcile the differences between strength and humility?

#87 Some portion of the leading we do might best be described as, "Well . . . somebody's got to!" There are some things that no one else seems willing to tackle. If you ever really wanted to feel like "somebody," then these are your moments. Lead on!

#88 Do you try to lead everyone you are responsible for in exactly the same way? If so, then you aren't maximizing your potential or theirs. And you are probably missing out on the ways in which some of your people need to be led.

#89 Too many of us look for excuses. Too few of us look for opportunities. For what are you looking? Why? What will it take for your vision to shift more positively?

#90 Do you think that having different leadership styles with different employees is inconsistent? Try leading them all in the same way and see how that works. Yes, you have to be yourself. But within that selfhood, some versatility will serve you (and them) well.

#91 "They" say balance in your life is not possible. "They" say that balance is for those who choose not to achieve. Who are "they" anyway? Whose rules are *you* playing by?

#92 So much of truth, energy, and possibility is discovered when things are operating in balance. Courage definitely becomes more likely when there is balance. For you, what does "balance" need to look like?

#93 One person's lazy is another person's balance. There is such a thing as *lazy*. But there is also *balance*, led by a healthy sense of "enough" and by a love for people and things other than work. What is your intentional mix of these ingredients?

#94 You do not have to neglect your home life for your work. You do not need to neglect the office for your family. But you may have to change jobs in order to achieve this kind of balance.

#95 There once was a gifted young executive who is a star performer. He is definitely an asset to his organization. However, to be a star in this particular setting is a liability to his marriage, his family life, and his health. He will die early, but he will be remembered as a star.

#96 A long-term sense of healthy balance in life does not preclude short-term seasons of imbalance. Be reasonable. Be committed. Be flexible.

#97 Most of us are wired to be more change-resistant than we realize. We are so eager to appear appearing flexible that we probably believe we really are. Yet many of us hold tightly and dearly to patterns and habits as well.

#98 "Most people are opposed to two things: change and the same old thing."
—Ben McDade

#99 Communicate your expectations, your questions, and your hopes on the front-end of a project. Be transparent, at least at the level that you trust your team. How you set up a process makes some of the moves you make later a little easier.

#100 There once was a leader who spoke freely and often about change. For years, impending change was promised. Alas, change was never defined exactly, and neither was the process for implementing change. The organization learned to live in constant anxiety and paranoia. Well, there once was a person who spoke freely and often about change. Turns out, this person wasn't much of a "leader" after all.

#101 People become nervous when change is discussed without specifics. Be careful how you engage the topic, taking care to monitor whether you have created opportunity or simply made people wary of you.

#102 Changing our behavior is difficult. We can develop a vision, evaluate, and calculate, all of which will suggest change that needs to happen. We can respond to these steps with designs and action plans. But our behaviors drive so much of what we do. Which behavioral ruts are you stuck in right now?

#103 When you delegate, make sure that all parties understand at the beginning that you might need to step back into the leadership role. Good communication is the key to good delegating.

#104 The most difficult math problem is adding up our blessings. In a culture of expectancy, we can be too focused on our failures and numbed to the gifts of God. Stop and look around you. Your life is better than you think!

#105 You are not your possessions. You are not your problems. You are not your job. You are not your failures. You *are* a person of worth filled with creative potential. How do you define yourself?

#106 Too many of us get caught up in looking around ourselves rather than looking inside ourselves. Yes, good things are happening to others. Yes, people around you are enjoying life. You have the same potential, and you have similar opportunities. Refocus your vision on who you are and who you are becoming.

#107 "Seems like yesterday, I was at work squabbling over an issue with a long-time friend. Seems like yesterday, his leukemia returned and he passed away. Seems like yesterday, we went from fussing about work to his passing. Yet again, a reminder that life is short. We need to embrace what we have, love the dickens out of it, and be thankful for every moment that we get. Seems like yesterday . . ." .
—From a personal friend of Charles

#108 Most people don't care how the "sausage" gets made. Most people are only interested in a higher quality "sausage" than the "sausage" factory down the street.

#109 Nobody really cares how much work you have to do. They really only care about how much work you get done and the quality of that work.

#110 If you are employed and provided for, gratitude is an appropriate response. Gratitude does not preclude having dreams of a new work-life chapter somewhere else someday. But until you arrive at that new place, you might consider how much gratitude is appropriate for where you are now.

#111 What you have done to this point should only be prelude to what you will do in the future. Never just stop where you are. What grand movement is next for you?

#112 A lot of people worry about self-care but aren't really doing much besides talking about caring for themselves. Do something each day that models for others self-care.

#113 Some of the younger generation employees have the self-care thing mastered. What they don't have mastered is the show-up-and-work thing. Balance assumes that we are doing a proper and healthy amount of more than one thing. Work hard and your self-care will be accepted by those around you.

#114 Too many of us worry that we are missing some opportunity. Too many of us worry that there is not enough time. Too many of us dwell on "woulda, shoulda, coulda" excuses. Focus on the blessings in your life. Focus on the opportunities that are before you. Perform to your best ability today!

#115 Do you work so hard because too much of yourself is tied to satisfaction and identity from your work? Okay, here is what you do: make a fist like you are going to knock on a door; go ahead, we'll wait. Now, raise that "knocking fist" to your forehead and rap lightly several times. Why? Because working *too* hard is never as noble nor as productive as we assume. Wake up and rebalance while you still can! (Repeat the knocking on your forehead as necessary.)

#116 A lot of people don't worry enough about self-care and aren't doing much besides working. There's nothing heroic about neglecting yourself, those who love you, or things that feed your passion in the name of earning a living.

#117 The need for balance in our lives is a healthy urge to follow. Don't overcorrect. Just evaluate and find a way to pull things back to your center. Extremes are rarely where health is found.

#118 Do you have a prayer list? Take a moment to begin one. Write down events in your life that need divine intervention. Write down people in your life who need divine intervention. Keep a running list and pay attention to how the divine is intervening in your life. You might be surprised . . . and blessed!

#119 "Out of suffering have emerged the strongest souls; the most massive character is seared with scars."
—Kahlil Gibran

#120 We all know from experience that running away from our problems does not solve them. Some would contend that trying to run from a problem only creates distance from a solution. Work through problems strategically and in a timely way. Get them out of the way so you can move forward.

#121 We learn in so many different ways. What will be instructive to one person will be lost on another. Figure out how you learn best, and use those ways to your advantage. Be a lifelong learner.

#122 At this writing, a popular saying is flying around on social media: "Life is hard; it's harder if you're stupid." Ponder your ability to make life a little easier and then act accordingly.

#123 Learn in the everyday. One of the greatest tragedies is when a person fails to notice that daily life is a campus of insight! Put this book down for a second and ask yourself, *What deep lessons can I learn from my experiences today?* Record your thoughts in the blank pages of this book.

#124 Examine your life every evening before bedtime: What lessons did I learn today? What blessings did I receive today? What blessings did I bestow today? Where did I see God in these lessons and the blessings?

#125 Albert Einstein supposedly said, "Anyone who has never made a mistake has never tried anything new." What mistakes are you making? What lessons are you learning? What new things are you trying?

#126 "Truth often suffers more by the heat of its defenders than from the arguments of its opposers."
—William Penn

#127 If you can't describe the process clearly and concisely to your stakeholders, you won't be able to build consensus. People will think you're not sure about what you're doing.

#128 Sometimes leaders have to do the hard things, the unpleasant things. Sometimes leaders have to confront bad behavior and deal with difficult situations. Sometimes leaders just have to set up tables and chairs for a meeting. Each day has its own challenges.

#129 The value of our experience is found in what we've done with what has happened to us. Having life knock us around is not to be confused with experience.

#130 As of this writing, our culture seems to be consumed with customizing and individualizing truth. As a leader, you had better know what you hold to be truth. These bedrock values and convictions will be tested, but they will also guide your accomplishments.

#131 Do not compromise on truth. There are other things you can compromise; let truth not be one of them. What are the core truths that drive your life.

#132 A daily prayer might be, "Lord, help me to remember that all the truth I recognize is not *all* the truth."

#133 Just because you are ready to have the difficult, awkward, or shocking conversation does not mean the other party is. Bring others along with you to the bigger moments. If you have surprised and upset someone, your message may not be as effective as you had hoped.

#134 Is your faith bigger than your fear? This question might be the gateway to some good introspection. What does God want you to do that challenges you?

#135 Some of our most challenging calls from God will not make headlines. Many of those "ordinary" tasks are woven into our daily lives and happen as we are going about our business. While you are thinking big, be sure that you remember to do the small things well. This may be difficult and challenging.

#136 "See that justice is done, let mercy be your first concern, and humbly obey your God." Micah 6:8

#137 "If one dream should fall and break into a thousand pieces, never be afraid to pick one of those pieces up and begin again."
—Artist Flavia Weedn

#138 Someone once said that a rut is just a grave with both ends kicked out. What keeps you fresh and creative? In what ways do you do more than just survive?

#139 There once was a leader whose vocabulary included the phrase "I want." This had traveled with her since childhood. When, as a leader, she did not know how to tame this voice, she sometimes violated fairness with her team. Her "want" became one of her greatest weaknesses.

#140 How might you apply this bit of wisdom to your life? "Yesterday is gone. Tomorrow has not yet come. We have only today. Let us begin."
—Mother Teresa

#141 "Faith is taking the first step, even when you don't see the whole staircase."
—Martin Luther King, Jr.

#142 Going through the motions is *never* good enough! If that's the best you can do, don't!

#143 Silence really is golden. If you are angry, be silent. If you don't know what to say, be silent. If you don't know how to respond appropriately, be silent.

#144 Don't be tempted by the all-you-can-eat buffet! You can't eat it all! You can't have it all. Choose wisely. More than 60 percent of us are overweight! Remember the English proverb, "Enough is as good as a feast."

#145 People complain. People complain when they're too comfortable. And when they're uncomfortable. When things happen too slowly. And when things happen too quickly. When memory fades. And when life is overly romanticized. When they're hungry, thirsty, hot, cold—breathing! People complain.

#146 When people complain, they also seek to place blame. Don't be trapped by their complaints, their blame—or their praise.

#147 No matter how good things may be, there is always someone who is going to complain, effectively throwing cold water on goodness. Listen selectively!

#148 We can no more control the future than we can erase the past. All we have is the grace and joy of today. Learn what you will today to have an impact tomorrow.

#149 Today is the tomorrow that worried you yesterday—and all is well!

#150 These are "the good old days." The past too easily lures us; the future too easily frightens us.

#151 Don't get so caught up in your ego that you think you alone are the reason for your successes or your blessings. Forsake not the higher power at work in your life!

#152 Work doesn't kill us. Food doesn't kill us. Ego doesn't kill us. What is killing us is the lack of discipline in a moderated lifestyle.
—Anonymous

#153 "To be early is to be on time, to be on time is to be late, to be late is to be left behind."
—from Bo's friend, John Mark Bowes

#154 Take some time to play. Creative energy is generated by play. Ride a carousel, race go-karts, play a round of golf (or putt-putt). Go to a movie, read a book to escape, go for a hike. Find time to play!

#155 If you *think* all you know is all you *need* to know, you don't know all there is to know. What *else* do you need to know? Who can help you begin to know?

#156 What are you doing as a leader to engage your team? You can't expect people just to show up energized. You have to engage them with energy that motivates them to participation.

#157 When you do well, have the dignity to win with humility. Win humbly, lose graciously, and you'll always be a winner.

#158 What is the best lesson that "losing" has ever taught you? What is the best lesson that "winning" has ever taught you? Which experience is the better teacher?

#159 What are your top five wildest dreams? What's keeping you from achieving even one of these? Write down your top five, keep them accessible, and stay motivated to achieve.

#160 Who are your role models and mentors? Have you ever thanked them? If not, perhaps take a moment to send a note of thanks. For whom can you be a role model or mentor?

#161 Take a moment to pray, placing your hand over your heart and feeling "life" pulsing through your body. Pay attention to your breathing and feel "life" entering your body. Say a word of thanks to the creator, God, and feel "life" flowing all around you.

#162 If you are average, you are as close to the bottom as you are to the top. Risk being more! It's really loneliest in the middle!

#163 Courage brings an energy that is its own reward. The courage to take smart risks is never classified as failure, regardless of the outcome!

#164 There once was a leader who took unnecessary risks just for the adrenaline rush. The leader never achieved anything except an addiction to adrenaline. This was not courageous or strategic, mostly just foolish. What is your addiction? Are you a leader or just adrenaline junkie?

#165 We hear lots of people say, "I'm spiritual but not religious." Others say, "I'm religious but not very spiritual." We say, "We are both spiritual and religious! Spirituality leads us to community and religious practices. Religion leads us to deeper spirituality. It's difficult to be one and not the other if we are growing."

#166 Fear is a waste of energy. The Scriptures are filled with the admonition "Fear not!" Move forward with confidence.

#167 When was the last time you exercised? In a land of overweight people, twenty minutes a day can keep you feeling more mentally energized, emotionally upbeat, and physically fit .

#168 What gets measured gets done! Who holds you accountable in your money management, in your work, in your marriage, in your parenting, in your leadership? What about in your eating and exercise habits? Is it time to consider consulting a personal trainer or financial guide?

#169 Who is your favorite musician? Spend twenty minutes today listening, really listening, to their music. Let this be your "quiet time" today, paying attention to the honesty of the lyrics. Perhaps write down a thought in the back of this book that connects with you.

#170 Who is your favorite comedian? Spend twenty minutes today listening, really listening, to their comedy. Let this be your "quiet time" today, Write down a thought in the back of this book that connects with you.

#171 "If your ship doesn't come in, swim out to meet it!"
—attributed to comedian Jonathan Winters

#172 Your idea will not be everyone else's idea. Nor will your way always be the best one. A willingness to listen and learn is, over the long haul, a quality that your team will appreciate.

#173 Your idea may be the best idea. If you only listen to the ideas of others, you'll lose the discipline of original and creative thought for yourself.

#174 When you are "in the zone," keep the energy and effort going. When you are in a slump, grab hold of the energy around you and restart. Neither the "zone" nor the slump is permanent. Enjoy the positive energy of one, and overcome the negativity of the other.

#175 The people you lead need to know that you care about them, as people, colleagues, friends. When they sense your investment in their lives, getting them to share ideas is much easier. How do you demonstrate your investment in those you lead?

#176 Paying one's dues seems to be viewed as an archaic practice of the past. Of course, this mindset is espoused by a generation that also struggles to gain entry into professional work streams. We all pay our dues along the way, one way or another. There is no place for entitlement in today's workplace. How have you "paid your dues"?

#177 Paying your dues will not end as you attain veteran status in your profession. Each change of setting or level will involve a learning curve. Use this dues-paying wisely!

#178 How do you know if the culture within your organization has grown toxic? Trusted individuals who have permission to "shoot straight" with you are vital to your leadership. If you can't trust them, find someone you can. If they can't trust you—thus ends the mystery as to whether the culture in your organization has grown toxic!

#179 As we react to bad news or hardship, responses of shock or even denial may kick in. These defenses are not our enemies. Just be careful how long you allow yourself to grieve and struggle. Listen to the healthy voices around you (and within you) that will eventually help you to wake up and move on.

#180 Taking in sounds is not enough. People need evidence that we hear them. Listen actively using your eyes as well as your ears. Give appropriate feedback. You are not obligated to agree; you are obligated to listen.

#181 In one church, a particular lady would say, "You just don't ever listen to me!" One day, I thought to say in return, "Oh, I do listen to you. It's just that I don't often agree." That wasn't what she wanted to hear, but in that moment we did communicate. How do you reassure others that they are heard?

#182 Listening in no way obligates you to agree. In fact, you will often need to disagree for the good of the organization. But listening is the beginning of honest communication.

#183 If you are new to an organization, one of the first commodities you will need is a trustworthy "historian" to give you an honest appraisal of what's what! Seek understanding about what is past, what is sacred, and of whom you need to be mindful.

#184 Jesus calls us to love. That much is evident throughout the New Testament. But so much of our loving is action. So much of our loving is also choice. How does love weave its way into your leadership?

#185 Many of us approach leadership as a journey toward being something. We forget that our team is really first interested in who we are. If we want to become something of greatness, we must be someone of *goodness* first.

#186 *Loving* does not always equate to *liking*. Once you accept that you are called to love all—but not necessarily required to like all—your loving may become easier. How do you understand the differences between these two?

#187 Good leaders share the credit for every good thing the team accomplishes.

#188 The key to everything is good relationships. Whether you are at work or at home, relationships are at the center of your world. Human interaction is at the center of everything. How are you fostering positive relationships?

#189 There is someone on your team who is underutilized. This person is rarely noticed or is perhaps even marginalized. People don't invest in them; they don't see their gifts. Untapped potential is here. You are the leader. What will you do with and for this person?

#190 Among the classic buzzwords in leadership are "efficiency" and "maximization." Well, get to maximizing. Be strategic enough to place each person on your team in a position where she or he can succeed.

#191 Leadership involves traits that are both innate and learned. Much of what we see as a weakness can be developed into strength. Which leadership skills are innate to you? Which have been learned?

#192 You may have tendencies and patterns that you rely upon consistently, but that doesn't doom you to be stuck in them. Look for new and refreshing ways to express yourself and your talents.

#193 Do you have a mentor? We learn in different ways and from different personality types.

Find a figure whose work and style you admire. Learn from them.

#194 Experience can be a wise instructor! But only inasmuch as the student is paying attention. We can do things poorly, and do them poorly for a long time. And we can also pay attention and improve. Take advantage of your experience.

#195 Strong leaders know there is much to learn from the collective wisdom of mentors and experienced colleagues. How do you welcome such insights and offers of help?

#196 Did you do anything that mattered today? Why or why not? "Worshipful work" must be more than answering e-mail, opening "snail" mail, and returning phone calls. Are your work hours an offering to the divine? What needs to change?

#197 Meditate on this question, "Where are you?" Allow your meditation to lead you deeper into the intersection between your heart and the heart of the Divine. But, don't stop at mediation, once you discover, *act*!

—Trevor Hudson

#198 Courage has been defined in various ways. One very good definition is that courage is knowing what lies around the next corner and then making the turn anyway. What corner do you have just ahead? What corner do you dread turning? What are you doing to prepare for the turns that await you?

#199 What are the strengths you bring to your workplace? God has made you unique. Lead from your strengths, even while working to shore up your "growing edges."

#200 Some of the strengths that make us good in the workplace may make us rather weak in relationships at home if we overplay those strengths. Your spouse is not the next deal to be closed, and your best friend is not the next opponent to be outfoxed. They don't like feeling as though they are being played or managed, and they won't likely give you forever to realize that!

#201 Envy is an emotional scourge. Envy will sap the life out of your confidence and your graciousness. We should admire the special qualities and accomplishments of others, but when we lapse into envy, we lose our ability to be happy for others. That is an unhealthy place from which to lead.

#202 We live and relate in patterns. Know your patterns. Some of them work. Others don't and need to be interrupted. You can do some things differently. You really can. So, what might your needs be?

#203 "Emotional intelligence" is a quickly emerging field of understanding. We all have our strong points. But we have dimensions of how we relate that could be improved. Are you open to knowing yourself better? Are you open to growing and changing?

#204 Emotional intelligence is the ability to perceive, understand, evaluate, and appropriately express emotions. This happens instinctively. Pay attention to the emotions that rage within you and around you. Respond appropriately.

#205 We only really deal with four main emotions: happiness, sadness, anger, and fear. Some add one more: confusion. Every other emotion is a combination of one of these. What are you feeling right now? What are you going to do with the emotions you now recognize?

#206 A former president adopted and used the axiom, "Trust, but verify." Jesus said, "See, I am sending you out like sheep into the midst of wolves; so be wise as serpents and innocent as doves" (Matt 10:16, NRSV). Fine counsel, both of them.

#207 Here are some of the ingredients that build trust: a track record of doing the right thing consistently, a sense that you can hold on to confidential information and insights, good character that guides you in other peoples' big moments, and decisions that demonstrate a greater good at heart.

#208 What keeps you from trusting? No doubt, past experience. Maybe some of your socialization is thrown into the mix, too. Sooner or later, though, you have to risk something. Be wise but not paralyzed!

#209 The church owes its people a word of apology about forgiveness. In our zeal to teach the grace of Christ, we have made forgiveness sound like a transaction that happens like the flip of a light-switch. Get real with your impasses! Do the work of truly forgiving.

#210 The hard work of forgiveness is worth doing, because the pain that leads us to the need to forgive imprisons us until we do. True forgiveness may have even less to do with the other person than with us.

#211 Forgiveness is important for us to achieve, because moving forward is ultimately impossible until we have shed the weight of hurt that holds us back.

#212 Spending a little extra time on the "how" part of your communication could be an investment that pays off. You can downgrade exactly the right message with exactly the wrong approach. By knowing your audience (even an audience of one!), you can maximize the impact of what you hope to say.

#213 You will not become a great leader without being a great communicator. They cannot be separated any more than pen can be from ink. Or should that be "printer from cartridge." Well, you provide the analogy . . .

#214 Are you focusing on the right things in your work? Unless you focus on the right things for the right reasons, you'll never be pleased with what you achieve. What are the right things? Well, you'll have to decide, but my hunch is that "rightness" has something to do with serving others before yourself.

#215 Communicating opinions, analysis, and vision carries greater risk than information generally will. If you ask coworkers for their insights, be sensitive to your response to what they share. Respect their investment and honor their risk, even when there turns out to be disagreement.

#216 You cannot control how accurately you are heard. You can control how accurately you communicate information. You have a responsibility to assess whether or not you have been heard accurately.

#217 Recognize multiple types of intelligence. Use your strengths, but do not be seduced into thinking that your gifts are the greatest. Someone nearby has other equal gifts, even if not as obvious to you.

#218 The best decision maker on your team may not always be the quickest. Address those who mistake thoughtfulness, or thoroughness, with indecisiveness.

#219 Sometimes the best decision is the one that carries you forward into action. You may not yet be able to see all you'd like to see ahead. The blanks that are not filled in may have to wait.

#220 Surround yourself with good people who are skilled enough to be honest with you and each other. Keep each other out of possible bad habits and affirm each other into good successes.

#221 Hiring based only on skill set may not pay off in the long run. Instead, hire for good attitude, even if the skill set needs some coaching. A team player is valued for more than their skills.

#222 If things are moving too slowly for your comfort, speed up the process. If things are moving too quickly for your comfort, slow down the process. If things are chaotic, add more structure. If things are too structured, loosen up a bit. Bottom line: be flexible!

#223 What holds you back from making a decision? Your issue might be fear or lack of confidence. Perhaps you see so many options that all opportunities seem good. Someone in your orbit can help you over the hump when you are stuck. Will you let them?

#224 A visionary decision maker can sit in the ashes of failure and begin to determine the next move forward. Others? They just sit in the ashes and lament.

#225 Trusting your gut is often the best edge you have. In an era of measurement and predictive metrics, sometimes you still have to lead by the best "feel" you have for a situation.

Many of those good hunches are born of experience and would never test out in a study or a forecast.

#226 In reality, we need all kinds of leaders. That's because we have all kinds of followers. Even the most decorated of leaders have someone they follow.

#227 Are you so suspicious of others that you trust no one? Are you certain that every flattery is really a maneuver and that every compliment is a ploy? You will find that trusting others pays off more than it betrays you.

#228 No one truly arrives! Even the most accomplished in our world must keep pushing to achieve and become more. Enjoy the journey or drive yourself crazy.

#229 If having money is the only focus of your life, you'll never have enough. Focus instead on those priorities of life that will make you truly rich.

#230 All of those people you are too wise to trust? Yep, they have learned not to trust you, too! How do we know? Because you taught them. Learning to trust others builds trust and teaches others to trust you more!

#231 Avoid discussing any misgivings about one employee with another. Pretty soon, your team members will wonder what you say about them when they are not around.

#232 It is important to know when to take—and when to share—control. What tasks and decisions need to be shared with your staff? What tasks and decisions uniquely need your hands-on action?

#233 When we carry responsibility and a situation demands action, we must find a way to lead. In a vacuum, followers will begin to fill that void with all manner of ideas. Some of them might be good, but many of them will not.

#234 Life and work will present speed bumps along the way. Don't let a speed bump be converted into a dead end. Some people can't tell them apart! Find another way around; become creative at calculating a new route!

#235 "Obstacles either polish us up or wear us down. A diamond was just a hunk of coal until it was put under pressure and polished to perfection."
—Mary Kay Ash

#236 You have failed at some point. That does not make you a failure. What that does do is leave you altered in some way. Get to know that difference, for you will never be quite the same again.

#237 The things in life that have wounded you can be platforms for learning. Put forth the effort of collecting the lessons with clarity. Process those lessons. Write about your experience. Emerge stronger once the healing has begun.

#238 You will never completely leave behind the memory (and pain) of your worst failures. The words and scenes will replay themselves occasionally. This is not necessarily the worst thing. But don't get stuck here! Keep moving forward!

#239 No one wants to hear your complaints. Nor will they credit you many excuses. Dispense complaints in needful doses, because you only get so many. After that, you're simply viewed as a whiner.

#240 When you delegate, do so to the right person at the right time. That can save a lot of heartache down the road. This seems obvious, yet many of us struggle with the results of bad judgment after our delegation fails.

#241 There once was a leader who was jealous of other leaders. No matter how much he was capable of, he could not get past his own envy. He really wasn't much of a leader at all.

#242 There once was a leader who was trusting of other leaders. For every success her colleagues achieved, she was there to cheer them on and celebrate their accomplishments. She really was a great leader.

#243 The "great recession" that began in roughly 2008 has given most of us something to think about. Suddenly, our standards of the *ideal* job or the *best* workplace got a healthy dose of perspective. A job in hand sure does beat one we don't have. Appreciate your ability to make a living. Appreciate an organization that seems to want you.

#244 A little secret: "workaholism" is almost always a way of avoiding something. Very few of us just love our work that much. What are you scared of going home to? What do you fear might be exposed at the office if you were away?

#245 You are far less good to your organization if you are ill. Is your workload robbing you of basic health? Interrupting "toxic" work habits may be harder than you think. Set attainable goals for yourself each day. Take a walk for about five minutes. Speak to three people in the office each day. Concentrate on your breath prayer. Do something to keep yourself mentally, physically, and spiritually healthy.

#246 You are of no good to your organization if you have grown to resent the company. If so, take time to enjoy other aspects in your life that leave you feeling healthier and happier. The irony is, if your company is not all you have in your life, you will be better postured to give yourself to it as needed.

#247 "Failure should be our teacher, not our undertaker. Failure is delay, not defeat. It is a temporary detour, not a dead end. Failure is something we can avoid only by saying nothing, doing nothing, and being nothing."
—Denis Waitley

#248 Debriefing projects, even for those projects that have gone well, serve a valuable purpose. This doesn't take long but can leave behind a helpful to-do list for next time and can help us all reinforce valuable universals for other types of projects.

#249 When an employee leaves your organization, is there any arrangement made for exit interviewing? There is a lot we may not want to hear. But there is a lot that we need to hear.

#250 If you have moved a work project from an employee and made other arrangements for that project to be completed, debrief the "why" with the employee. Both of you might learn something from what could seem like a touchy-feely waste of time.

#251 Be very careful to have sorted out the difference between what truth is and is not. Truth may not be one and the same with your biases, your customs, your assumptions, and your folkways!

#252 "When things are falling apart they may be falling together."
—Unknown

#253 Do you run from conflict? Few of us truly enjoy trouble with other people, but conflict will be a part of our lives if we are doing much of anything. Be careful how powerfully the instinct to avoid conflict is informing your leadership. Being in touch with what is driving you will serve your organization well.

#254 Have you known people who were addicted to a mild amount of conflict? They gain energy by raising the anxiety of others. Good leaders should develop strategies for identifying and diffusing workplace drama.

#255 There is a fundamental difference between being brave and being reckless. It comes back to knowing yourself and knowing what is driving you. Some things that might appear bold on the surface really turn out to be needlessly reckless. Are you angry? Feeling the need to win one? Your brave plan could just be reckless. Live to fight another day.

#256 Someone has said that courage is not the absence of fear. Instead, courage is knowing that a challenge is coming and embracing the challenge anyway. We may experience a season where we have to lead with deep courage. Overcoming challenges gives us courage for the next ones.

#257 Do you prefer texting to talking? Technology has made it very easy to avoid actually speaking to one another. Be mindful of occasions in which you ought to shift your communication from texting or e-mailing to a phone call or a face-to-face meeting.

#258 Do not allow the habits of the digital age dictate your mode of communication. Be sure you are communicating clearly. What works electronically may not always work in person.

#259 Five minutes on the phone can save an hour of e-mailing back and forth. Do whatever it takes for clear and accurate communication to happen!

#260 The digital age of communication has brought about so many different ways to reach each other. Hold tight to a sense of boundaries. Just because you can reach your team members does not mean you always should. If the idea comes after hours, have the discipline to wait.

#261 Sometimes we need to have the wisdom to say, "That would have been a great idea . . . if I had thought of it in time." Last-minute emergency changes are costly and less efficient than strategic thought. Plus, "emergency thinking" eventually wears out the creativity of the team.

#262 The improvisational leader has the energy to move from disappointment to disappointment without losing the enthusiasm to keep trying.

#263 The improvisational leader finds ways to say "Yes . . . and" in every situation. When we say no, we effectively squelch communication and creativity.

#264 If you are a leader, you have people around you who will give in to you if you push them. However, at what cost will some of your victories come? Be mindful of how you burn your resources. And your team members are resources!

#265 When you are engaged in a conversation, much more is happening than just "talk." The relationship, however insignificant or important, is always being added to or subtracted from. Pay attention to the debits and credits in your relationships.

#266 To say that relationships are at the center of our leadership sounds too mushy for some. However, relationships really are the currency of our leadership. If that sounds like something you are uncomfortable with, you may be exactly the person who needs to invest more in those with whom you work.

#267 There is a fundamental difference between "knowing" and "discerning." Discernment is the mental, emotional, and spiritual activity of going beyond simply "knowing."

#268 At a certain point in life, few things satisfy quite like tying down the proverbial "loose ends." One also learns that not all loose ends need to be tied down. Both things are true. Know the difference.

#269 Take a day once a month or so for "housecleaning." Clean up your office and tidy your work area. Go through a file drawer and throw away dated files and old teaching materials. Nothing feels better than to clean up, throw away, and clear out.

#270 Some of us are pack rats. Overflowing files drawers and outdated electronic files get in the way. Keep one hard copy of old training materials. Keep electronic files for three to five years. Each time you update training materials, delete the old file. Clear away the clutter that clogs up your storage facilities.

#271 The kitchen table is the most family-friendly place in the home. This space is in danger of being ignored as we eat meals on the run, use it for our home office, and eat meals in front of the television or in the minivan. Spend intentional times at the kitchen table. No electronics allowed, no television, no radio, and no distractions. Your family will thank you (eventually); you heart will overflow.

#272 The kitchen table is the place for important discussions too. Set a timer for five minutes and have each family member write down questions they need answered from other family members. (If you have younger children, let them color or do a puzzle while everyone else is writing.) After five minutes, spend time discussing one another's questions, sharing information, coordinating schedules, and laughing together. Close the "meeting" with sentence prayers from each family member.

#273 Electronic media is continuing to encroach on face-to-face interaction. Declare a media-free night once a week in your home. Institute "No E-mail Fridays" in your office. Set some times when you turn off the electronic "leashes" to which many of us are attached.

#274 One night a week must be declared as "date night" for you and your spouse or for you and special friends, if you're not married. Have fun with these evenings, and be creative. These don't have to be elaborate events but rather fun times for you and your spouse (or friends) to escape for a bit. Your spouse will thank you; your friends will thank you.

#275 Resolution is a powerful moment in life. Some things in your organization's life need to be resolved. Soon! What project needs to be brought to a fruitful conclusion? What project needs to be shut down even without conclusion? There is great freedom in stopping some things and ending others.

#276 One leader likes to speak up occasionally and say, "It's time to land the plane!" When the moment arrives, do you know how to bring the project, speech, or meeting in for a safe and timely landing? When you do, people are energized. When you don't, a crash is sure to happen.

#277 Someone once said, "He's a gifted speaker and a smart guy. If only he knew when to end his presentations! He consistently delivers three different endings." Know when to stop. Know when to be quiet.

#278 Perhaps knowing how to end is more important than know how to start. We often tell speakers, "Edit, edit, edit! It is hard to be bad if you're brief." You have three to five seconds to create interest. You have four to six minutes to maintain interest. You have about twenty-two minutes to start, shift, and end without losing your audience.

#279 Conflict is inevitable. You have no control over that. What you do have control over is how and when you approach conflict. When others are backing away from conflict, the leader will be the one who steps forward.

#280 Sometimes the obstacle that requires our greatest courage does not register on paper as a big deal at all. By conventional measures, some of our nightmares seem like nothing. Ask yourself what makes you truly *anxious*? This may be an obstacle that requires your greatest courage.

#281 When we do the thing we thought was impossible, we bank up courage for the future. Life helps us grow one experience— one victory—at a time. What have you not done that you must do soon? What's keeping you from action? Take courage!

#282 Are you as flexible as you need to be? We're not talking about your physical flexibility; this is about your work habits. Times change and ways of working change. Will *you* change?

#283 Spend time with social media. Learn how to use technology for communicating clearly and effectively. The tools are there for a broader audience, so use them to share your message.

#284 Start a blog. Think of this as an electronic journal. Blogging is easy, fun, and a good discipline. Once a week, write four paragraphs about one idea. Don't tell everything you know about everything, just write a reflection about something you find yourself thinking about. You'll enjoy the process. Others will enjoy your thoughts.

#285 Don't believe adequate talent surrounds you? Are you lamenting the terrible luck of who is on your team? Stop! The responsibility is upon you as a leader. How will you guide them toward improvement? How will you deploy them to tasks they can be effective doing?

#286 Shuffle the job tasks for your team members. Put all the job tasks and responsibilities on a white board and let team members choose their work. Let them tell you what they do best and what challenges they'd like to try.

Then rewrite job descriptions and responsibilities to fit the people on your team.

#287 Every job has its difficult aspects. That's why it's called "work." If we enjoyed every part of our work, it would be called "fun"!

#288 Mistakes get made. Things happen that weren't planned for. Occasionally things go wrong. How you react will tell your team a lot about your character. Too little reaction is one problem. Too much reaction is equally unsettling.

#289 The shelf life on our formal education or training is frighteningly short. How do you continue to be informed, stay current, and challenge your thinking? Incorporate a blend of self-education, peer or mentor coaching, and structured learning into your routine. You'll need all three to keep your edge.

#290 Skill sets are important in all of our jobs. Even if you might be tempted to think that your work does not involve skill as much as expertise or information, don't kid yourself.

The relational and communicative aspects of our work consist of skills. Keep current and stay sharp.

#291 Emotional intelligence is comprised of a lot of skills and aptitudes, including active listening, impulse control, empathy, and the ability to communicate assertively. In all, there are more than a dozen basic ones. These can be worked on and strengthened.

#292 You are not stuck where you are unless you choose to be. You always have options for growth and learning. Consult a career counselor, talk to a personal counselor, seek out a trusted mentor. Grow for it!

#293 What is the best thing you have *not* done in a long time? That's right. Ask yourself what is the best thing you (or your organization) have been ignoring. Then ask why. If there is no good reason, think about whether or not the time is right to begin doing that "best" thing again.

#294 Who you keep company with says a lot about you. The actions you have already taken say a lot about you. So, if you are trying to move forward, take a glance sideways and backward. Vision for action comes to us in many directions.

#295 There once was a talented leader; no, that's not entirely accurate. He was talented, but he had no self-confidence to lead. He didn't really know himself well and did nothing to become self-aware. Okay, there once was a talented person who failed to live up to even a fraction of his potential. A shame, really.

#296 We all know the person who simply can't stay out of her own way. She is a good person. She has redeeming qualities. But hardship travels with her. We should learn from her: how do you seem to get in your own way?

#297 At the end of the day, we really are our own worst enemies. The biggest frustration in life is when there is no one to blame but yourself.

#298 "When your life is a never-ending series of overly dramatic events; at some point, you should consider that you have taken on the role of the lead character!"
—Anonymous

#299 One piece of advice that one of our senior adult friends has passed along: "Make the most of a bad job." Nearly all of us will have one along the way.

#300 Even if what you are learning is about how not to do things, you are still learning. Pay attention to life lessons and bank your wisdom.

#301 Find work that is fulfilling. Do you wake up dreading to go to the office? You should listen to that. Some people have reinvented their roles at a particular job. Others have changed jobs. What do you need to do?

#302 Our greatest regrets are likely to come from what we did not do. What is pulling or tugging at you in your soul? What risks are you pondering? Listen to these voices, especially if you are young.

#303 Choose wisely whom you will trust. Sometimes grace suggests that we will trust again someone who has already burned us.

#304 Many of us know how to "do," but fewer of us know how to "be"! Lots of us are people of action. Fewer of us are people of reflection. Take time to just "be" today.

#305 "Confidence on the outside begins by living with integrity on the inside."
—Brian Tracy

#306 People often ask us what the difference is between a leader and a boss. The leader works in the open with transparency. The boss is more covert and less transparent. The leader leads and the boss drives.

#307 "Progress is not made without some risks. You can't steal second base with your foot still on first base."

—Anonymous

#308 "Telling the truth may not always get you the most friends, but it will get you the right friends."

—Anonymous

#309 There is a difference between truth telling and bluntness. Be sure you know where the line is, and stay on the healthy side of it. You may not have ultimate responsibility for how people receive your communication, but you do have full responsibility for your intentions.

#310 Integrity is a staple of leadership. If you say it, mean it. If you mean it, do it! Over time, this will be something more people will notice than just about any other trait.

#311 If you work on an active, creative, and assertive team, there will eventually be *hurt* to deal with. Creative processes that lead to newness will occasionally push across the edges of territory and assumption. Expect forgiveness to be a part of your workplace.

#312 A popular movie line once spawned a pop-culture mindset: True love means never having to say you're sorry. There is only one problem. It was "movie life," not "real life"! In real-life relationships, you often have to say you're sorry, especially if you care deeply about people.

#313 The improvisational leader is one who refuses to compete with his or her team members about ideas. We are always looking for the best ideas, regardless of who generates them.

#314 The improvisational leader is one who builds consensus and is not one who sets up competitions. What are you doing to foster team spirit and build community?

#315 If we change jobs each time there is hurt or dissonance, we will ride a never-ending trolley of employment. Dig down and do things the tough but lasting way. Do the work of resolution or reinvention.

#316 No matter how much you accomplish or how well you do, there will always be critics and naysayers. Pay them no mind. Doing well is your best response.

#317 Live in the moment. Don't get too far ahead of the process. Don't celebrate or become discouraged too early. Stay focused; work the process.

#318 Some say that I am weird or odd. I say I am unique! Life is all in how you look at it.

#319 I am not special, entitled, or privileged. However, I am very blessed. Today I hope to live even more into the blessings God has bestowed upon me. What about you?

#320 There is a difference between "entitlement" and "opportunity." One assumes a guarantee and privilege; the other assumes hard work and potential. Which do you assume? Be careful!

#321 Wealth and power can entice and intoxicate. Pay attention to how a higher power is leading you, blessing you. Stay humble!

#322 What is that *one* thing that you love to do and are passionate about? How much time are you spending doing this? Spend time each week doing what you love; you will be energized for other tasks.

#323 It's hard to be bad when you are brief. Think, "I only have a limited number of words. How can I best use these to communicate clearly and succinctly?" When blogging, be brief too. Think, "One idea, four paragraphs."

#324 When designing projected visuals, be brief too. Think, "No more than five lines of copy, no more than five words per line. One picture equals two lines of copy."

#325 How do you successfully adhere to a limited use of words? One word: edit, edit, edit!

#326 Did you give your all today or just do enough to get by? How you answer may reflect how passionate you are about your work.

#327 Babies can teach us a lot about leadership: if something stinks, change it!

#328 If getting fired is the worst that can happen, what might be the least that can happen? What are you worrying about again?!

#329 Fear can motivate or stagnate. The way you respond determines how you will lead.

#330 Where humans are gathered, there will be brokenness. Our organizations—even the non-profit world—will feature hurt feelings and disappointments. What will we do with that disillusionment? What we do determines how effective and how lasting we will be in service to those who need us.

#331 We can "talk past the sale," as one personnel expert likes to say. Sometimes more words simply are not needed. At some point, action and time tell the rest of the story.

#332 Your words really do have strength and power. Consider very carefully how you use them. Do not be shy when that power is called for; do not be a bully when a gentler touch is better.

#333 There can be too few words; there can be too many. Be aware of yourself. Be aware of your words. Know when to be quiet. Know when to speak.

#334 One editor friend likes to say, "You never fix a problem with more words." We can learn something from this print-journalism axiom. How does this apply to your practices of communication?

#335 Another editor friend says, "Don't do battle with the one who owns the ink!" We can learn from this axiom. Pick your battles wisely!

#336 Great communicators are aware of the place and the moment. This subtlety of emotional intelligence is lost on some otherwise very gifted people. A leader knows the setting, the context, and the subtleties.

#337 Great communicators know their audience. There once was an invited speaker who began name-dropping. But the names he was dropping were people whose ideas were philosophically opposite of his audience. He was the only person in the room who didn't realize that he had killed his own moment.

#338 Peace of mind is priceless, but it cannot be the determining factor in every decision. Peace of mind helps you sleep at night. Sometimes a tough decision keeps you awake!

#339 A leader is decisive when decisiveness is called for. Some people are naturally more reflective in their reactions. Others become paralyzed trying to gather consensus. When you need to, can you move quickly and emphatically?

#340 Your team will naturally want quick answers from you. When you are not responsive quickly, they may view you as indecisive. But sometimes the quickest answer may not be the best one. Be disciplined, but not *stuck*.

#341 Be careful about the false deadlines that you (and others) impose. We can find ourselves racing some clock or calendar that is a false taskmaster. Be intentional about what and who is driving you!

#342 When you make a decision, take just a minute to make sure that your motives are pure and that you've decided with integrity. If so, then trust it all the more. If not, then keep wrestling until you can be sure.

#343 How powerful a driver is *fear* in your decisions? "What am I afraid of?" is a very distilling question. There are legitimate fears in life. Then there are all the paralyzing fears. Be smart enough to know the difference.

#344 Do you have a mentor who particularly reflects Jesus to you? If so, asking yourself what your mentor might do is not a bad question. Better yet, sit down with your mentor and ask!

#345 Don't feel obligated to deny your losses. Everyone has had them. No one will believe the words—or the image—of the one who acts as though they've never lost.

#346 The winner who crawls across the finish line is still a winner.

#347 A good leader wants to do more than just the job. A good leader strives for excellence. Do you take things to a level of excellence, whatever that may mean? Or do you settle for just getting on to the next task?

#348 Be sure there are people on your team who believe in you. Believing in you is not the same as always agreeing with you. Free them to be honest *and* supportive.

#349 Sometimes you have to make it a great day. If you don't, nobody (and nothing else) will.

This sounds clichéd, but our attitudes really are powerful shapers of how our days go.

#350 Empower those to whom you delegate. If you haven't equipped, trained, and permitted, you have simply increased the likelihood of failure.

#351 In taking back work that someone has failed to accomplish, timing will be important. Sometimes leaders hesitate for all the right reasons. Still, this hesitation may cause worse problems down the road. Be decisive and fair.

#352 Do you give your workplace your best? Or do you do something quite different, namely, work hard in order to be valuable so that your career will advance. These truly are two different approaches. Ironically, both of them often lead to those advancement opportunities. But one of these is better for all parties involved.

#353 When we are as invested in our organization as we are to ourselves, very powerful things can happen in our work. What do you see when you look into the mirror of your conscience? Paperclips are not the only commodities that we can steal from our companies. Are you invested?

#354 All leaders need someone who journeys with them for the long haul. This is someone who knows them and "gets" them, someone who will support them in tricky times and just plain tough times. This is also someone who will celebrate the victories with them.

#355 Being a lone-wolf leader is a tough person to be. This life not only is lonely but also is difficult on your coworkers and those you would lead. The lone-wolf is difficult to know and even harder to trust.

#356 A ringing phone does not have to be answered if you are in the middle of something important. The phone is one of the most powerful interrupters we have if we allow that to happen. Control your phone or your phone will control you.

#357 Does your listening feel like it obligates you to say *yes* all the time? Listening is one thing. Going along with what seems expected is quite another. Being able to make people feel heard without having to give in to everything "everybody" wants is crucial. "No" is part of your responsibility. "Yes" is part of your privilege.

#358 Are there things no one prepared you for in your work? That is true for all of us. In fact, what we do with the unknown is a powerful indicator of our creativity as leaders.

#359 Are you bored with your job? Bored with your surroundings? Bored with the people you work with? Then you are probably about to make costly mistakes. You do not have the luxury of boredom. Get excited or get a new job!

#360 Bored at your workplace? Find a way to rebuild either your job or yourself at that job. Negotiate with others if need be. How can you reinvigorate what has become stale? Innovation and purpose can be tools that make the old become new!

#361 There is confusion about honesty and openness. The line between an honest leader and someone whose bluntness is destructive can be elusive. If you pride yourself on your honesty, then examine the sensitivity with which you use this trait. Honesty and unnecessary bluntness really aren't the same thing.

#362 In the search for responsible strategy, many of us err toward secrecy. You can disclose too much. But you can just as easily disclose too little. Find the line between openness and discretion.

#363 One minister said of another, "He is one of the most gifted young fellows I have seen in a while. But I don't think he's very self-aware. And that's his weak spot. Sometimes, he just doesn't know when to stop talking." God has presented us with the holy gift of knowing when to be quiet.

#364 When others know you are holding back on them, you will only add animosity to whatever outcome you were fearing. If you insist on holding out, you had better have your team's trust.

#365 "Don't do something permanently stupid just because you're temporarily upset."
—Unknown

#366 "Individual commitment to a group effort—that is what makes a team work, a company work, a society work, a civilization work."
—Vince Lombardi

#367 "Is God leading you into a frightening season? An adventure for which you feel ill-equipped and unprepared? Remember, the CALL of God will never take you where the GRACE of God will not sustain you."
—Shaun Michael King

#368 "A credible witness is one who stakes an unshakable claim in the truth, even when others have disregarded it."
—Barry Howard

#369 What is driving you? In marriage and divorce work, this is a key question. So, too, in any of our work. If you are being driven by unhealthy or irrational issues, those issues need some work. Beware when your leadership pays too high a price for your own personal issues.

#370 There are situations where wisdom calls for the art of being purposefully vague. Learn this, and use it not as subterfuge but as a discipline.

#371 You have heard the saying "It doesn't matter so much what you say as how you say it." Well, don't believe that so deeply! Because the truth is that both things matter greatly. Your message needs to be as "on point" as your delivery.

#372 Delivering accurate and helpful criticism or advice will not be enough. How you deliver this content will matter just as much. Maybe more. Be careful to know how the people you work with best receive communication.

#373 There is simply no good way to deliver some news. "You've let me down." "You're fired." "There's been a death." When we have to deliver bad news, news that stings, show your human side. A little empathy goes a long way.

#374 Have you ever been to a Hawaiian luau? The fire dancers are spellbinding. We marvel at their skill and the ease with which they do things. Ever seen one of those people up close? Yep . . . scars. We can learn something from them about our own woundedness.

#375 Every organization needs someone who can come out of their regular role to work in the role most needed. As a leader, know who that might be. Call on them when needed, but monitor their own fulfillment so that you keep them satisfied.

#376 Risk-taking will come with the mantle of leadership. There is no effective leader who has managed to stay entirely on safe ground. On the contrary, your loneliness at times just comes with the territory. The risky moments can be isolating. Expect this.

#377 The tested leader will have some scars to show for their resumé: lines in the face from worry, scars on the hands from working; a woundedness of spirit that informs how they do things. This is to be expected, but does not, in and of itself, buy you credibility.

#378 Do people know what to count on from you? A leader who keeps her team guessing is a confusing leader. Consistency is not to be confused with rigidity or sameness. Flexibility does not rule out a steadiness that defines.

#379 There are simply going to be times when the wheels come off! No matter how hard you've worked, no matter how sound your reasoning or strategy, sometimes things just go bad. What you do in the face of that hard reality says a lot about you as a leader.

#380 Avoiding trouble or misfortune is not the true test of a leader. No one is good enough or smart enough to dodge troubling times forever. Never mind crisis. Let yourself be human. Let yourself have a future by moving on from the past.

#381 Be careful what you pray for. Work out your faith journey fearfully and imaginatively! Without ceasing.

#382 If at first you don't succeed:
A) Quit
B) Try a different approach
C) Ask for help
D) Enlist an expert
E) Enlist someone who knows nothing about the issue
F) Refer to another group
There is no right answer; they are all options that may be appropriate.

#383 Find ways to appeal to the natural curiosity of a group. There are aspects of any project that naturally appeal to group members. Allow their curiosity and creativity to shape planning and production.

#384 Think short-term results while considering long-term implications. Remember, long-range planning is six weeks to three months in today's climate!

#385 Post a thought on Twitter and Facebook every day. What to post? One of these motivators, of course! Or some of your own!

#386 Play a game of free cell, Sudoku, or work a crossword puzzle everyday. Give yourself a time limit to deepen the challenge!

#387 Ask yourself, "What's the worst that might happen?" Rarely does the worst-case ever happen. Don't let any other negatives pull you off course!

#388 "Good enough is the biggest obstacle to great!"
—Jim Collins

#389 Perfection is the biggest obstacle to action. Do "it" perfect next time!

#390 Write a thank-you note daily to someone who has had a positive impact on your life.

#391 Understand that you don't know everything about everything. All the truth you know is not *all* the truth!

#392 Take someone interesting to lunch once a week. Ask them to share three keys to being a good leader.

#393 Don't neglect the work of a higher power influencing your work, your journey, and your passion.

#394 If you're too busy to care for people, you need to reevaluate your schedule.

#395 Make space for the holy to have an impact on your pace of life.

#396 Don't allow negative people to derail your journey. Twenty percent of the people in your organization are against everything!

#397 Rarely is the negative talk about you. You may be the lightning rod, but stay the course of positive action.

#398 The anxiety and negativity in a leadership team represent that of the larger system. Be aware of the negative feelings, confront these when appropriate, and keep on task.

#399 You can't control any situation or any person. You can control how *you* respond to the situation or person.

#400 Prayer and meditation keep you focused, intentional, and better able to negotiate obstacles, endure challenges, and respect others.

#401 Don't be enamored by those who praise you or discouraged by those who criticize you. Keep your ego in check and stay focused on your goals.

#402 The best advice from yesterday: "Don't do it today if you don't want to read about it in the newspaper tomorrow." The best advice from today: "Don't do it today if you don't want to see it in social media immediately or viral on the Web!"

#403 Take care of your body! When tired, you don't control your emotions well; you don't make good decisions.

#404 Preconceived notions block creativity, worshipful work, and deeper relationships. Come to each new setting, meeting, or gathering as a blank canvas.

#405 Build a culture that is challenging enough to foster change yet safe enough to build deep relationships. These two factors will lead to strong consensus building.

#406 Negativity is never productive. Keep finding ways to move with positive energy in every situation.

#407 Ministry and leadership are all about relationships. Who are your leaders? Who are your team members? Who needs your friendship?

#408 Never forget that there is a higher power at work in the universe. God is in control. Use your influence for the greater good!

#409 No matter how well you plan, something will go wrong. Roll with it! Don't get sidetracked by it.

#410 Much of what we do is spontaneous. Respond, react, rejoice!

#411 The things we haven't done or didn't do keep us awake at night. Do the most important things first and keep working with intentionality.

#412 Take care of your physical body and emotional self in the same way that you take care of spiritual self.

#413 Sometimes you have to do the things you don't want to. Sometimes you have to endure things to get to do what you want to do.

#414 Sometimes helping someone ultimately hurts them. Be wise enough to know whether your helping is really helping or hurting.

#415 Stuck on what to preach? Go clean the kitchen sink! And pray! Still stuck, go mow the lawn or take a nap. Keep praying!

#416 Stuck on whom to serve? Go wash your hands! And pray! Still stuck, go ride around your community, pay attention. And pray! When we get stuck, doing the mundane often brings about revelation!

#417 "Whatever you bind on earth will be bound in heaven, and whatever you loose on earth will be loosed in heaven" (Matt 16:19). Live into abundance!

#418 Technology can be your friend or your enemy. Don't try to learn everything about every piece of software. Develop your suite of technology tools and learn to use these effectively and efficiently.

#419 Social media may be the biggest time waster in your suite of technology tools. Spend your time wisely on social media sites. You cannot read everything posted by everyone. Choose wisely who you will follow and whose writings you will follow.

#420 Spend "chunks of time" with technology and social media. Limit yourself to blocks of time during the day. Be disciplined with your time.

#421 Don't use social media to tell everything you know or everything you are doing. Most people aren't that interested.

#422 If you are writing a blog, don't try to write a book with each post. Generally, think about your blog posts in the form of "one idea, four to five paragraphs." Brief and pertinent thoughts get read.

#423 Work in ways that people know what you're doing, with whom you're ministering, and how you're spending your day. Trying to explain yourself is a waste of energy. Your friends don't expect it and your critics won't believe it.

#424 Every day holds opportunities for learning. Don't waste your time with frustration and ambivalence. Continue asking yourself, "What is this event teaching me? What is this experience guiding me toward? How is this event blessing me?"

#425 The more positive you can keep your attitude, the more effective you are as a leader. Discipline yourself to stay focused on the good things that are happening around you.

#426 Quit looking backwards. Learn from the past and leave it. The more time you spend in the past, the less time you have for living in the present . . . for action in the here and now, moving beyond "what used to be."

#427 Quit looking forward. Anticipate the present and live into it! The more time you spend in the future, the less time you have for living in the present . . . for action in the here and now, getting ready for "what's next."

#428 There is a fine line between good enough and great. Good enough keeps us from achieving greatness.

#429 Don't settle for less than excellence—but be careful with seeking perfection. Do it with excellence this time; perfection may come next time!

#430 Not everything will work out the way you planned it! Be flexible, adjust, and adapt. Most of what we worry about rarely happens! The "worst that could happen" rarely does!

#431 Try being silent for thirty minutes a day. Give God some holy space and time to get your attention.

#432 "If I were in this business only for the business, I would not be in *this* business."
—Filmmaker Samuel Goldwyn

#433 When receiving feedback, the key is to depersonalize the input. Feedback is constructive not destructive. Listen, learn, implement, and move on.

#434 "I don't look to jump over 7-foot bars: I look for 1-foot bars that I can step over."
—Investor Warren Buffett

#435 How resilient and adaptable are you? Resilience comes from continually adapting and adjusting and enjoying the process.

#436 One of your greatest duties as a leader is to inspire and encourage those with whom you work. If you are not confident in this ability, practice, practice, practice.

#437 Interruptions and unplanned interactions are not necessarily time wasters. Pay attention to these as necessary "touches" that keep you connected to what is really important.

#438 The career ladder is very challenging. Build on your experiences and don't expect to start at the top. Pay your dues, live intentionally.

#439 Follow your dreams. You may not always achieve your dreams, but you have to keep pushing for accomplishments and special moments.

#440 What is your guilty pleasure? When is the last time you enjoyed your guilty pleasure? Take some time this week to pamper yourself, enjoy a bit of life, and celebrate the goodness of the blessings that abound.

#441 Your team is filled with enthusiasm and pessimism. The challenge is for you to release one and defeat the other. How can you encourage your team to develop enthusiastic energy?

#442 "It's kind of fun to do the impossible."
—Walt Disney

#443 Money follows mission. Carefully and clearly define your mission and people will support you with resources and participation.

#444 Money follows excellence. Focus your mission and then perform with excellence. Those who believe in you will continue to support you as you perform with excellence, quality, and value.

#445 Enticing others to support your dream depends more on how you appeal to their interests and emotions rather than their intellect.

#446 Good people are developed by the wisdom they've gained by coming through bad experiences. Bad experiences come from a lack of wisdom. It seems like a vicious circle unless you are paying attention and learning!

#447 Nothing proves a person's ability to lead others better than the daily indications of personal discipline and self-direction.

#448 Develop avenues for feedback that are honest and sensitive. Brutal feedback does nothing to help anyone. Honest feedback helps you depersonalize the information and move forward constructively.

#449 Fear of failure inhibits excellent performance. Encourage team members to keep reaching for excellence. Continually reaffirm your support for your team and let them know you have their "backs"!

#450 Everything ultimately comes down to the strength of relationships. People are your greatest asset.

#451 Various athletic and corporate coaches will tell you, "The will to win is important to success. However, the will to prepare for winning is even more critical. Failing to prepare is failure regardless of the outcome."

#452 Courage is contagious. Courage helps those who practice it and those who benefit from courageous practice.

#453 One of the best practices for leadership is learning how to ask good questions. Focus on who, how, and what.

#454 Learn from the "best practice" of the legal profession: never ask a question for which you don't already know the answer. This takes practice, attentive listening, and persistence.

#455 A staff that is formed simply to get a job done will work hard to achieve results. But a staff that is formed around shared beliefs will be passionately invested in achieving results.

#456 Trust your gut. Intuition is a wonderful gift that you can rely upon daily. Pay attention to what your intuition is telling you.

#457 Being smart is not about how much you've memorized, how much you know, or even test scores. "Smart" is the ability to recognize the difference between what you know and what you don't know and how to ask for help.

#458 Think creatively for a moment:
What does red taste like?
What does green smell like?
What does blue sound like?
Have fun asking some "colorful" questions.

#459 Perhaps there is no better way to get team members to talk to you than by being silent. Practice being silent; see what happens.

#460 "It's not who you know, it's who knows you."
—Jeffrey Gitomer

#461 "There will come a time in everyone's career when they have to endure adversity. If you are lucky, this happens early, you learn from it, and move forward with resillience."
—Jim Morgan, CEO of Krispy Kreme

#462 Facts and data inform creative action and improvisation. The improvisational leader is not flying blindly but acting in the moment with decision that are informed by research and thought.

#463 Waiting for something to happen may be the worst kind of agony. Be proactive; engage your context by aggressively involving yourself in the setting where you find yourself. The outcomes may not be what you wished, but at least you influenced the process.

#464 Be attentive to meetings and times. Ten minutes early is on time, arriving at the scheduled time is late, and arriving ten minutes late is unforgivable!

#465 There is nothing quite like the serenity of sunrise and sunset. Take time to give yourself the gift of both of these! Listen to the sounds, breathe in the smells, and pay attention to the holy.

#466 One day a week, focus on personal relationships. Take a friend to lunch, write cards of encouragement and affirmation, enjoy time with yoru spouse, best friend, family.

#467 Self-pity is a waste of creative energy. When you are tempted, get up and do something constructive for others.

#468 You are uniquely capable of being creative and responding appropriately. Lead passionately with confidence.

#469 Those who aren't dwelling on the effect they have on others are usually surprised by how much of an effect they have. Those who think themselves important rarely are.

#470 Humility is usually a good choice. Be confident and be humble!

#471 Do what you truly, deeply, and passionately care about. Money and accomplishment rarely come without passion. And if money and accolades don't come, there is reward in the passion alone.

#472 Pay attention to "art" and "craft." One will help you work with excellence; one will help you deliver with pizazz!

#473 The question is not "Why is this happening *to* me?" The question should be "Since this is happening to me, what am I going to do?" There are opportunities in every situation; the challenge is to pay attention to them.

#474 Just because everyone around you panics does not mean that you should too. Learn how to live in a less anxious way than those around you. Just because they think the sky is falling does not make it so.

#475 Pay attention to the cultural norms around you. Be aware of the sports teams in your area. Be aware of the politics in your area. Be aware of the trends and fads in your area. We can't reach the people around us unless we understand the context in which we live and work.

#476 Spend a few minutes of your day with social media. Connections, even virtual ones, are important. Don't post what you had for dinner; do post some truth that has had an effect on you. If you can't think of your own post, use one of these motivators!

#477 Spend a few minutes of your day with television or music. Give yourself permission to relax, listening to your favorite artist or watching your favorite show. Some wise person once warned us about "all work and no play"!

#478 Difficult choices do not get any easier when we ignore them or delay dealing with them. Face the tough decisions head on with honesty and confidence. The sooner you make a hard decision, the sooner you can begin turning negative energy into positive outcomes.

#479 Procrastination only gives others the opportunity to act. The more you put things off, the more you open yourself up for others to decide. Engage your world your way. Take the initiative with integrity and energy.

#480 Give joy to all those around you. Practice generosity. Practice affirmation. Practice intentionality. All the joy that you share will come back to you multiplied beyond your imaginings.

#481 Technology is a wonderful tool. However, technology can also be a distraction. Don't get so engrossed in the Internet, social media, phone applications, and all the rest that you get distracted from your main purposes. Keep the main thing the main thing.

#482 Nothing works better than effort. As you exert effort, you achieve. Don't sit and hope for some "magic bullet" to success. Don't sit and wait for some fairy god-person to make your dreams come true. Get up right now and put forth some effort toward your goals, hopes, and dreams. Purposeful effort will fill you with energy, enthusiasm, expectations, and rewards.

#483 Fear can either paralyze you or prepare you. You decide! Regardless, fear makes you more aware of the situation and conditions around you. But don't stay stuck in the fear. Once the fear has brought you to awareness, plan, prepare, and produce!

#484 The world is moving on parallel tracks simultaneously. As things are getting larger, things are getting smaller. As things are running faster, things are running slower. As things are increasing, things are decreasing. "Macro" and "micro" are happening together, at the same time, all around us.

#485 Who are the "fruitcakes" around you? How do you respond to their insanity? Rather than writing them off or ignoring them, learn from them!

#486 The invisible affects the visible. The values, integrity, and beliefs inside you are what influence your behavior, productivity, and actions. Spend some time every day centering yourself, caring for the "invisible you," and living into the positive.

#487 The speed and purpose that you exert will be mirrored in your team. We all lead by example; our team members are watching for our reactions. The intentionality with which the team responds will be equal to or greater than the intentionality of your leadership.

#488 "I've learned that you can't have everything and do everything at the same time."
—Oprah Winfrey

#489 We all have within us four styles of leader: a rules-follower, a politician, a cheerleader, and a team player. The way we interpret any situation will determine which style of leader emerges from within us. The only "wrong" style is the one we use all the time.

#490 Pay attention to the big problems. The big problems take up energy. But pay attention to the small problems, too. The small problems can add up and sap your energy just as much as the big problems. Stay focused, stay intentional, stay in problem-solving mode.

#491 Choose joy! When you choose to live in joy, you choose to share your joy with those around you. Yes, there are reasons to be discouraged, but that doesn't mean you must be discouraged. Choose to live with joy and you will create plenty of reasons to be joyful. As you share joy, the joy is multiplied within you, around you, and toward you.

#492 "They may forget what you said but they will never forget how you made them feel."
— Carl W. Buechner

#493 "I am still learning."
— Michelangelo

#494 Sometimes the best approach is to apologize and move on. Better to apologize and save a friendship than to let pride be an obstacle and lose a friend.

#495 Saying thank you is a good spiritual practice as well as good manners. Don't miss any opportunity to express thanks to those who do nice things for you. Make gratitude a natural expression of your life.

#496 Sometimes you can play "both ends against the middle" to gain information. Just make sure you are not in the middle when things begin to squeeze!

#497 Stay above the fray by staying less anxious. Don't let the "drama" infect you and your team.

#498 When you feel tension, stress, or anger, analyze why you are having those feelings. Your mind can help you manage the intensity of your feelings and more appropriately express them.

#499 When was the last time you spent doing something you truly love? Today is the day; now is the moment. Close this book, turn off your computer, go out and do something that truly excites you and makes you feel truly and fully alive.

#500 When situations are tense, try being silent. There is no better way to ease anxiety than silence. Practice being silent in the midst of tension and see what happens.

#501 Practice silence. How?
A. Do nothing
B. Think nothing
C. Embrace nothing
D. Plan nothing
E. Just be! It takes practice but is well worth it!

Now it's your turn. On the pages that follow, jot down some of your own motivators. Add to the book, make it your own. Highlight motivators that excite and inspire you. Mark pages to which you want to return. Let us know what you're thinking and how you're motivating yourselves. We're on Facebook, so keep us posted!

Other available titles from  Smyth & Helwys

Beyond the American Dream
Millard Fuller

In 1968, Millard finished the story of his journey from pauper to millionaire to home builder. His wife, Linda, occasionally would ask him about getting it published, but Millard would reply, "Not now. I'm too busy." This is that story. 978-1-57312-563-5 272 pages/pb **$20.00**

The Black Church
Relevant or Irrelevant in the 21st Century?
Reginald F. Davis

The Black Church contends that a relevant church struggles to correct oppression, not maintain it. How can the black church focus on the liberation of the black community, thereby reclaiming the loyalty and respect of the black community? 978-1-57312-557-4 144 pages/pb **$15.00**

Blissful Affliction
The Ministry and Misery of Writing
Judson Edwards

Edwards draws from more than forty years of writing experience to explore why we use the written word to change lives and how to improve the writing craft. 978-1-57312-594-9 144 pages/pb **$15.00**

Bottom Line Beliefs
Twelve Doctrines All Christians Hold in Common (Sort of)
Michael B. Brown

Despite our differences, there are principles that are bedrock to the Christian faith. These are the subject of Michael Brown's *Bottom Line Beliefs*. 978-1-57312-520-8 112 pages/pb **$15.00**

Christian Civility in an Uncivil World
Mitch Carnell, ed.

When we encounter a Christian who thinks and believes differently, we often experience that difference as an attack on the principles upon which we have built our lives and as a betrayal to the faith. However, it is possible for Christians to retain their differences and yet unite in respect for each other. It is possible to love one another and at the same time retain our individual beliefs.

978-1-57312-537-6 160 pages/pb **$17.00**

To order call 1-800-747-3016 or visit www.helwys.com

Choosing Gratitude
Learning to Love the Life You Have
James A. Autry

Autry reminds us that gratitude is a choice, a spiritual—not social—process. He suggests that if we cultivate gratitude as a way of being, we may not change the world and its ills, but we can change our response to the world. If we fill our lives with moments of gratitude, we will indeed love the life we have. *978-1-57312-614-4 144 pages/pb* **$15.00**

Contextualizing the Gospel
A Homiletic Commentary on 1 Corinthians
Brian L. Harbour

Harbour examines every part of Paul's letter, providing a rich resource for those who want to struggle with the difficult texts as well as the simple texts, who want to know how God's word—all of it—intersects with their lives today. *978-1-57312-589-5 240 pages/pb* **$19.00**

Dance Lessons
Moving to the Beat of God's Heart
Jeanie Miley

Miley shares her joys and struggles a she learns to "dance" with the Spirit of the Living God. *978-1-57312-622-9 240 pages/pb* **$19.00**

The Disturbing Galilean
Essays About Jesus
Malcolm Tolbert

In this captivating collection of essays, Dr. Malcolm Tolbert reflects on nearly two dozen stories taken largely from the Synoptic Gospels. Those stories range from Jesus' birth, temptation, teaching, anguish at Gethsemane, and crucifixion. *978-1-57312-530-7 140 pages/pb* **$15.00**

Divorce Ministry
A Guidebook
Charles Qualls

This book shares with the reader the value of establishing a divorce recovery ministry while also offering practical insights on establishing your own unique church-affiliated program. Whether you are working individually with one divorced person or leading a large group, *Divorce Ministry: A Guidebook* provides helpful resources to guide you through the emotional and relational issues divorced people often encounter.
978-1-57312-588-8 156 pages/pb **$16.00**

To order call **1-800-747-3016** or visit **www.helwys.com**

The Enoch Factor
The Sacred Art of Knowing God
Steve McSwain

The Enoch Factor is a persuasive argument for a more enlightened religious dialogue in America, one that affirms the goals of all religions—guiding followers in self-awareness, finding serenity and happiness, and discovering what the author describes as "the sacred art of knowing God."
978-1-57312-556-7 256 pages/pb **$21.00**

Faith Postures
Cultivating Christian Mindfulness
Holly Sprink

Sprink guides readers through her own growing awareness of God's desire for relationship and of developing the emotional, physical, spiritual postures that enable us to learn to be still, to listen, to be mindful of the One outside ourselves.
1-978-57312-547-5 160 pages/pb **$16.00**

The Good News According to Jesus
A New Kind of Christianity for a New Kind of Christian
Chuck Queen

In The Good News According to Jesus, Chuck Queen contends that when we broaden our study of Jesus, the result is a richer, deeper, healthier, more relevant and holistic gospel, a Christianity that can transform this world into God's new world.
978-1-57312-528-4 216 pages/pb **$18.00**

Healing Our Hurts
Coping with Difficult Emotions
Daniel Bagby

In Healing Our Hurts, Daniel Bagby identifies and explains all the dynamics at play in these complex emotions. Offering practical biblical insights to these feelings, he interprets faith-based responses to separate overly religious piety from true, natural human emotion. This book helps us learn how to deal with life's difficult emotions in a redemptive and responsible way.
978-1-57312-613-7 144 pages/pb **$15.00**

Hope for the Thinking Christian
Seeking a Path of Faith through Everyday Life
Stephen Reese

Readers who want to confront their faith more directly, to think it through and be open to God in an individual, authentic, spiritual encounter will find a resonant voice in Stephen Reese.
978-1-57312-553-6 160 pages/pb **$16.00**

To order call 1-800-747-3016 or visit www.helwys.com

Hoping Liberia
Stories of Civil War from Africa's First Republic
John Michael Helms

Through historical narrative, theological ponderings, personal confession, and thoughtful questions, Helms immerses readers in a period of political turmoil and violence, a devastating civil war, and the immeasurable suffering experienced by the Liberian people.

978-1-57312-544-4 208 pages/pb **$18.00**

A Hungry Soul Desperate to Taste God's Grace
Honest Prayers for Life
Charles Qualls

Part of how we *see* God is determined by how we *listen* to God. There is so much noise and movement in the world that competes with images of God. This noise would drown out God's beckoning voice and distract us. We may not sense what spiritual directors refer to as the *thin place*—God come near. Charles Qualls's newest book offers readers prayers for that journey toward the meaning and mystery of God.

978-1-57312-648-9 152 pages/pb **$14.00**

James (Smyth & Helwys Annual Bible Study series)
Being Right in a Wrong World
Michael D. McCullar

Unlike Paul, who wrote primarily to congregations defined by Gentile believers, James wrote to a dispersed and persecuted fellowship of Hebrew Christians who would soon endure even more difficulty in the coming years.

Teaching Guide 1-57312-604-5 160 pages/ pb **$14.00**
Study Guide 1-57312-605-2 96 pages/pb **$6.00**

James M. Dunn and Soul Freedom
Aaron Douglas Weaver

James Milton Dunn, over the last fifty years, has been the most aggressive Baptist proponent for religious liberty in the United States. Soul freedom—voluntary, uncoerced faith and an unfettered individual conscience before God—is the basis of his understanding of church-state separation and the historic Baptist basis of religious liberty.

978-1-57312-590-1 224 pages/pb **$18.00**

To order call **1-800-747-3016** or visit **www.helwys.com**

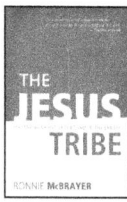
The Jesus Tribe
Following Christ in the Land of the Empire
Ronnie McBrayer

The Jesus Tribe fleshes out the implications, possibilities, contradictions, and complexities of what it means to live within the Jesus Tribe and in the shadow of the American Empire.

978-1-57312-592-5   208 pages/pb   **$17.00**

Joint Venture
Jeanie Miley

Joint Venture is a memoir of the author's journey to find and express her inner, authentic self, not as an egotistical venture, but as a sacred responsibility and partnership with God. Miley's quest for Christian wholeness is a rich resource for other seekers.

978-1-57312-581-9   224 pages/pb   **$17.00**

Let Me More of Their Beauty See
Reading Familiar Verses in Context
Diane G. Chen

Let Me More of Their Beauty See offers eight examples of how attention to the historical and literary settings can safeguard against taking a text out of context, bring out its transforming power in greater dimension, and help us apply Scripture appropriately in our daily lives.

978-1-57312-564-2   160 pages/pb   **$17.00**

Looking Around for God
The Strangely Reverent Observations of an Unconventional Christian
James A. Autry

Looking Around for God, Autry's tenth book, is in many ways his most personal. In it he considers his unique life of faith and belief in God. Autry is a former Fortune 500 executive, author, poet, and consultant whose work has had a significant influence on leadership thinking.

978-157312-484-3   144 pages/pb   **$16.00**

Maggie Lee for Good
Jinny and John Hinson

Maggie Lee for Good captures the essence of a young girl's boundless faith and spirit. Her parents' moving story of the accident that took her life will inspire readers who are facing loss, looking for evidence of God's sustaining grace, or searching for ways to make a meaningful difference in the lives of others.

978-1-57312-630-4   144 pages/pb   **$15.00**

To order call **1-800-747-3016** or visit **www.helwys.com**

Mount and Mountain
Vol. 1: A Reverend and a Rabbi Talk About the Ten Commandments
Rami Shapiro and Michael Smith

Mount and Mountain represents the first half of an interfaith dialogue—a dialogue that neither preaches nor placates but challenges its participants to work both singly and together in the task of reinterpreting sacred texts. Mike and Rami discuss the nature of divinity, the power of faith, the beauty of myth and story, the necessity of doubt, the achievements, failings, and future of religion, and, above all, the struggle to live ethically and in harmony with the way of God.   978-1-57312-612-0 144 pages/pb **$15.00**

Overcoming Adolescence
Growing Beyond Childhood into Maturity
Marion D. Aldridge

In *Overcoming Adolescence*, Marion Aldridge poses questions for adults of all ages to consider. His challenge to readers is one he has personally worked to confront: to grow up *all the way*—mentally, physically, academically, socially, emotionally, and spiritually. The key involves not only knowing how to work through the process but also how to recognize what may be contributing to our perpetual adolescence.

978-1-57312-577-2 156 pages/pb **$17.00**

Psychic Pancakes & Communion Pizza
More Musings and Mutterings of a Church Misfit
Bert Montgomery

Psychic Pancakes & Communion Pizza is Bert Montgomery's highly anticipated follow-up to Elvis, Willie, Jesus & Me and contains further reflections on music, film, culture, life, and finding Jesus in the midst of it all.   978-1-57312-578-9 160 pages/pb **$16.00**

Reading Job (Reading the Old Testament series)
A Literary and Theological Commentary
James L. Crenshaw

At issue in the Book of Job is a question with which most all of us struggle at some point in life, "Why do bad things happen to good people?" James Crenshaw has devoted his life to studying the disturbing matter of theodicy—divine justice—that troubles many people of faith.

978-1-57312-574-1 192 pages/pb **$22.00**

To order call **1-800-747-3016** or visit **www.helwys.com**

Reading Samuel (Reading the Old Testament series)
A Literary and Theological Commentary
Johanna W. H. van Wijk-Bos

Interpreted masterfully by preeminent Old Testament scholar Johanna W. H. van Wijk-Bos, the story of Samuel touches on a vast array of subjects that make up the rich fabric of human life. The reader gains an inside look at leadership, royal intrigue, military campaigns, occult practices, and the significance of religious objects of veneration.

978-1-57312-607-6 272 pages/pb **$22.00**

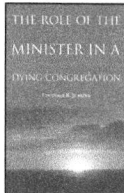

The Role of the Minister in a Dying Congregation
Lynwood B. Jenkins

In *The Role of the Minister in a Dying Congregation* Jenkins provides a courageous and responsible resource on one of the most critical issues in congregational life: how to help a congregation conclude its ministry life cycle with dignity and meaning.

978-1-57312-571-0 96 pages/pb **$14.00**

Sessions with Philippians (Session Bible Studies series)
Finding Joy in Community
Bo Prosser

In this brief letter to the Philippians, Paul makes clear the centrality of his faith in Jesus Christ, his love for the Philippian church, and his joy in serving both Christ and their church.

978-1-57312-579-6 112 pages/pb **$13.00**

Sessions with Samuel (Session Bible Studies series)
Stories from the Edge
Tony W. Cartledge

In these stories, Israel faces one crisis after another, a people constantly on the edge. Individuals such as Saul and David find themselves on the edge as well, facing troubles of leadership and personal struggle. Yet, each crisis becomes a gateway for learning that God is always present, that hope remains.

978-1-57312-555-0 112 pages/pb **$13.00**

Silver Linings
My Life Before and After Challenger 7
June Scobee Rodgers

We know the public story of *Challenger 7*'s tragic destruction. That day, June's life took a new direction that ultimately led to the creation of the Challenger Center and to new life and new love. Her story of Christian faith and triumph over adversity will inspire readers of every age.

978-1-57312-570-3 352 pages/hc **$28.00**

To order call 1-800-747-3016 or visit www.helwys.com

Spacious
Exploring Faith and Place
Holly Sprink

Exploring where we are and why that matters to God is an incredible, ongoing process. If we are present and attentive, God creatively and continuously widens our view of the world, whether we live in the Amazon or in our own hometown.

978-1-57312-649-6 156 pages/pb **$16.00**

This Is What a Preacher Looks Like
Sermons by Baptist Women in Ministry
Pamela Durso, ed.

In this collection of sermons by thirty-six Baptist women, their voices are soft and loud, prophetic and pastoral, humorous and sincere. They are African American, Asian, Latina, and Caucasian. They are sisters, wives, mothers, grandmothers, aunts, and friends.

978-1-57312-554-3 144 pages/pb **$18.00**

To Be a Good and Faithful Servant
The Life and Work of a Minister
Cecil Sherman

This book offers a window into how one pastor navigated the many daily challenges and opportunities of ministerial life and shares that wisdom with church leaders wherever they are in life—whether serving as lay leaders or as ministers just out of seminary, midway through a career, or seeking renewal after many years of service.   978-1-57312-559-8 208 pages/pb **$20.00**

Transformational Leadership
Leading with Integrity
Charles B. Bugg

"Transformational" leadership involves understanding and growing so that we can help create positive change in the world. This book encourages leaders to be willing to change if *they* want to help transform the world. They are honest about their personal strengths and weaknesses, and are not afraid of doing a fearless moral inventory of themselves.

978-1-57312-558-1 112 pages/pb **$14.00**

Written on My Heart
Daily Devotions for Your Journey through the Bible
Ann H. Smith

Smith takes readers on a fresh and exciting journey of daily readings of the Bible that will change, surprise, and renew you.

978-1-57312-549-9 288 pages/pb **$18.00**

To order call **1-800-747-3016** or visit **www.helwys.com**

When Crisis Comes Home
Revised and Expanded
John Lepper

The Bible is full of examples of how God's people, with homes grounded in the faith, faced crisis after crisis. These biblical personalities and families were not hopeless in the face of catastrophe—instead, their faith in God buoyed them, giving them hope for the future and strength to cope in the present. John Lepper will help you and your family prepare for, deal with, and learn from crises in your home.   978-1-57312-539-0   152 pages/pb   **$17.00**

Cecil Sherman Formations Commentary

Add the wit and wisdom of Cecil Sherman to your library. He wrote the Smyth & Helwys Formations Commentary for 15 years; now you can purchase the 5-volume compilation covering the best of Cecil Sherman from Genesis to Revelation.

Vol. 1: Genesis–Job   1-57312-476-1   208 pages/pb   **$17.00**
Vol. 2: Psalms–Malachi   1-57312-477-X   208 pages/pb   **$17.00**
Vol. 3: Matthew–Mark   1-57312-478-8   208 pages/pb   **$17.00**
Vol. 4: Luke–Acts   1-57312-479-6   208 pages/pb   **$17.00**
Vol. 5: Romans–Revelation   1-57312-480-X   208 pages/pb   **$17.00**

To order call **1-800-747-3016** or visit **www.helwys.com**

Clarence Jordan's
Cotton Patch Gospel

The Complete Collection

Hardback • 448 pages

Retail 50.00 • Your Price 45.00

The Cotton Patch Gospel, by Koinonia Farm founder Clarence Jordan, recasts the stories of Jesus and the letters of the New Testament into the language and culture of the mid-twentieth-century South. Born out of the civil rights struggle, these now-classic translations of much of the New Testament bring the far-away places of Scripture closer to home: Gainesville, Selma, Birmingham, Atlanta, Washington D.C.

More than a translation, *The Cotton Patch Gospel* continues to make clear the startling relevance of Scripture for today. Now for the first time collected in a single, hardcover volume, this edition comes complete with a new Introduction by President Jimmy Carter, a Foreword by Will D. Campbell, and an Afterword by Tony Campolo. Smyth & Helwys Publishing is proud to help reintroduce these seminal works of Clarence Jordan to a new generation of believers, in an edition that can be passed down to generations still to come.

 To order call **1-800-747-3016**
or visit **www.helwys.com**

www.ingramcontent.com/pod-product-compliance
Lightning Source LLC
Chambersburg PA
CBHW061440040426
42450CB00007B/1134